T0155243

9.7
DB2 ∦ for Linux, UNIX, and Windows Database Administration
Certification Study Notes

Roger E. Sanders

MC Press Online, LLC
Ketchum, ID 83340

DB2 9.7 for Linux, UNIX, and Windows Database Administration: Certification Study Notes
Roger E. Sanders

First Edition
First Printing—October 2011

© 2011 Roger E. Sanders. All rights reserved.

Every attempt has been made to provide correct information. However, the publisher and the author do not guarantee the accuracy of the book and do not assume responsibility for information included in or omitted from it.

The following terms are trademarks or registered trademarks of International Business Machines Corporation in the United States, other countries, or both: DB2, DB2 Connect, FlashCopy, IBM, Information on Demand, Optim, pureXML, and z/OS. A current list of IBM trademarks is available on the Web at http://www.ibm.com/legal/copytrade.shtml.
Linux is a registered trademark of Linus Torvalds in the United States, other countries, or both. UNIX is a registered trademark of The Open Group in the United States and other countries. SQL Server and Windows are registered trademarks of Microsoft Corporation in the United States, other countries, or both. Java and Oracle are registered trademarks of Oracle and/or its affiliates in the United States, other countries, or both. Other company, product, or service names may be trademarks or service marks of others.

Printed in Canada. All rights reserved. This publication is protected by copyright, and permission must be obtained from the publisher prior to any prohibited reproduction, storage in a retrieval system, or transmission in any form or by any means, electronic, mechanical, photocopying, recording, or likewise.

MC Press offers excellent discounts on this book when ordered in quantity for bulk purchases or special sales, which may include custom covers and content particular to your business, training goals, marketing focus, and branding interest.

MC Press Online, LLC
    Corporate Offices
    P.O. Box 4886
    Ketchum, ID 83340-4886 USA
For information regarding sales and/or customer service, please contact:
    MC Press
    P.O. Box 4300
    Big Sandy, TX 75755-4300 USA
    Toll Free: (877) 226-5394
For information regarding permissions or special orders, please contact:
    mcbooks@mcpressonline.com

ISBN: 978-1-58347-367-2

Contents

About the Author

Roger E. Sanders is a Senior Consultant Corporate Systems Engineer with EMC Corporation and president of Roger Sanders Enterprises, Inc. He has been working with DB2 9.7 for Linux, UNIX, and Windows and its predecessors since DB2 was first introduced on the IBM PC (as part of OS/2 1.3 Extended Edition) and has worked in the storage industry for the past 10 years.

Roger has written articles for *IDUG Solutions Journal* and *Certification Magazine*, authored DB2 tutorials for IBM's developerWorks Web site, presented at several International DB2 User's Group (IDUG) and regional DB2 User's Group (RUG) conferences, taught numerous classes on DB2 Fundamentals and Database Administration (DB2 for Linux, UNIX, and Windows), and is the author of 20 books on DB2 and one book on ODBC. For the past eight years, Roger has authored the Distributed DBA column in *IBM Data Management Magazine* (formerly *DB2 Magazine*), and he has helped IBM develop 17 DB2 LUW Certification Exams.

In 2008–2009, 2010, and 2011, Roger was recognized as an IBM Champion for Data Management. In 2010, he was recognized as an IBM developerWorks Contributing Author, and in 2011, he was recognized as an IBM developerWorks Professional Author.

Introduction

Shortly before my book *DB2 9 for Linux, UNIX, and Windows
Database Administration: Certification Study Guide* (MC
Press, 2007) went into a second printing (sometime in May 2009),
IBM invited me to help develop the DB2 9.7 for Linux, UNIX,
and Windows Database Administration (DBA) certification exam
(Exam 541). Knowing that a new version of the DBA exam was
about to be created, I contacted my editor and asked whether we
should update my DB2 9 book to cover the upcoming exam. At
that time, it was decided that such a revision would be too costly
and time consuming — that instead, the next revision would take
place after the DB2 10 exams were developed.

That same year, IBM invited me to, once again, teach my DB2 for
Linux, UNIX, and Windows DBA Certification Crammer course
at its Information On Demand (IOD) conference. And because
attendees would be able to take the 541 exam, at no charge, while
they were at the conference, IBM asked whether I could update
my training material and teach to the 541 exam. My answer
was "Yes," and I spent the next four to six weeks completely
reworking my training material to cover the 541 exam. I used the
same technique to develop the material for that course that I use
to develop all my certification exam training material and study
guides: I carefully reviewed the questions found on every version
of the certification exam, and I made sure that I covered the

topics test candidates would encounter when they attempted to take the 541 exam.

Starting around April of 2010, I began receiving emails from various individuals who wanted to know when I would have a study guide available for the DB2 9.7 DBA exam. My response always went something like this: "My publisher has decided not to do a book for the DB2 9.7 DBA exam. However, I will be teaching a class that will help you prepare for the 541 exam at the IDUG/IOD conference this May/October." This response almost always led to a request for a copy of my training material. But, because that material is copyrighted (and is, in fact, registered with the U.S. Copyright Office), I don't distribute it freely. So, unfortunately, I was unable to honor such requests.

Last year, after teaching my class at the 2010 IOD conference (where I once again was bombarded with questions about when a book for the 541 exam would be available), I approached my editor and made the suggestion that we make my training material for the 541 exam available, in the form of a supplement to the *DB2 9 for Linux, UNIX, and Windows Database Administration: Certification Study Guide*. She agreed, and the result is this book.

If you've bought this book (or if you are thinking about buying this book), chances are you've already decided that you want to acquire the DB2 9.7 for Linux, UNIX, and Windows Database Administrator Certification that's available from IBM. As an individual who has helped develop 17 IBM DB2 certification exams, let me assure you that the exams you must pass in order to become a certified DB2 professional are not easy. IBM prides itself on designing comprehensive certification exams that are relevant to the work environment to which an individual holding a particular certification will be exposed. As a result, all of IBM's certification exams are designed with the following items in mind:

- What are the critical tasks that must be performed by an individual who holds a particular professional certification?

- What skills must an individual possess in order to perform each critical task identified?

- How frequently will an individual perform each critical task identified?

You will find that in order to pass a DB2 certification exam, you must possess a solid understanding of DB2; for some of the more advanced certifications, such as the 544 exam, you must understand many of DB2's nuances as well.

Now for the good news. You are holding in your hands the *only* material that has been developed specifically to help you prepare for the DB2 9.7 for Linux, UNIX, and Windows Database Administration exam (Exam 541). When IBM began work on the 541 exam, I was invited once again to participate in the exam development process. In addition to helping define the exam objectives, I authored several exam questions, and I provided feedback on many more before the final exams went into production. As a consequence, I have seen every question you are likely to encounter, and I know every concept on which you will be tested when you take the 541 exam. Using this knowledge, along with copies of the actual exam questions, I developed these study notes, which cover every concept you must know in order to pass Exam 541. In short, if you see it in this book, you can count on seeing it on the exam; if you don't see it in this book, it won't be on the exam.

Where Are the Practice Questions?

For those of you who have purchased my DB2 certification study guides in the past, I would like to say thank you. A tremendous amount of effort went into the creation of those books, and it is rewarding to know that they are helping people become DB2-

certified. In addition to thanking you, I also want to comment up front about the absence in this book of sample questions and answers that you have grown to expect in my study guides. Because the pages that follow contain the slides I use to teach my DB2 for Linux, UNIX, and Windows DBA Certification Crammer course, there are no sample questions. And because I've been busy trying to finish the manuscript for my 23rd book — *From Idea to Print: How to Write a Technical Article or Book and Get It Published* — quite frankly, I did not have the time to create practice questions for this book!

With that said, I can promise you that you will find everything in the pages that follow that you must know in order to pass the 541 exam. If you become familiar with the material presented in this book, you should do well on the test.

Conventions Used

You will find many examples of DB2 administrative commands and SQL statements throughout this book. The following conventions are used whenever a DB2 command or SQL statement is presented:

[ ] Parameters or items shown inside brackets are required and must be provided.

< > Parameters or items shown inside angle brackets are optional and do not have to be provided.

| A vertical bar is used to indicate that one (and only one) item in the list of items presented can be specified.

,... A comma followed by three periods (ellipsis) indicates that multiple instances of the preceding parameter or item can be included in the DB2 command or SQL statement.

The following example illustrates each of these conventions:

```
UPDATE [DATABASE | DB]
[CONFIGURATION | CONFIG | CFG]
FOR [DatabaseAlias]
USING [[KeyWord] [Value] ,...]
<IMMEDIATE | DEFERRED>
```

In this example, DATABASE or DB is required, as is CONFIGURATION, CONFIG, or CFG; a *DatabaseAlias* value; and a *KeyWord-Value* pair, as indicated by the brackets ([ ]). In the case of DATABASE or DB, only one option can be specified, as indicated by the vertical bar (|). The same is true for CONFIGURATION, CONFIG, or CFG. More than one *KeyWord-Value* pair can be provided, as indicated by the comma-ellipsis (, . . .) characters that follow the *Value* parameter. IMMEDIATE and DEFERRED are optional, as indicated by the angle brackets (< >), and either one or the other, but not both, can be specified, as indicated by the vertical bar (|).

SQL is not a case-sensitive language, but for clarity, the SQL examples provided are shown in mixed case: command syntax is presented in upper case, while user-supplied elements such as table names and column names are presented in lower case. However, the examples shown can be entered in any case.

Note: Although basic syntax is presented for most of the DB2 commands and SQL statements covered in this book, the actual syntax supported may be much more complex. To view the complete syntax for a specific command, or to obtain more information about a particular command, refer to the *IBM DB2, Version 9.7 Command Reference*

product documentation. To view the complete syntax for a specific SQL statement or to obtain more information about a particular statement, refer to the *IBM DB2, Version 9.7 SQL Reference, Volume 2* product documentation.

● ●

1

DB2 Server Management

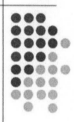

Ten percent (10%) of the DB2 9.7 for LUW Database Administration Exam is designed to test your knowledge of basic DB2 server management.

Servers, Instances, and Databases

DB2 9.7 sees the world as a hierarchy of objects. Workstations (or servers) occupy the highest level, instances occupy the second level, and databases make up the third level.

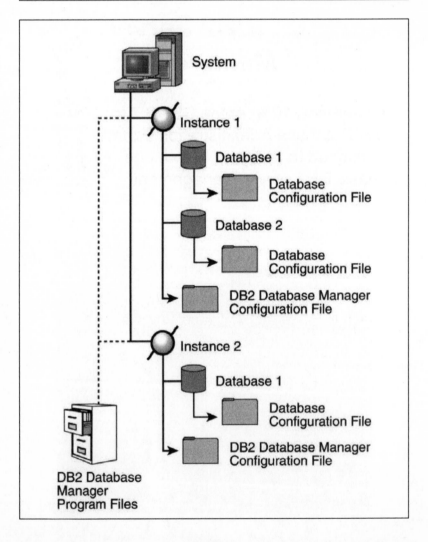

Configuring the DB2 System Environment

During normal operation, the behavior of a DB2 server is controlled, in part, by a collection of special DB2-specific system-level values. These values are stored in one of three different *environment* or *registry* profiles:

→ The DB2 Global Level Profile Registry
→ The DB2 Instance Level Profile Registry
→ The DB2 Instance Node Level Profile Registry

Values assigned to these registry profiles can be seen or set with the db2set command.

The db2set Command

```
db2set <[ Variable ] = [ Value ]>
<-g>
<-i [ InstanceName ] < PartitionNumber >>
<-all>
<-null>
<-r [ InstanceName ] < NodeNumber >>
<-n [ DASNode ] < u [ UserID ] <-p [ Password ]>>>
<-l | -lr>
<-v>
<-ul | -ur>
<-h | -?>
```

Examples of the db2set Command

`db2set`
Lists all registry variables that have been set for the current instance

`db2set -lr`
Displays a list of all registry variables that are supported by DB2

`db2set DB2_ATS_ENABLE=YES`
Enables the administrative task scheduler for the current instance

Configuring Instances

The behavior of a DB2 instance is controlled, in part, by a Database Manager configuration file. This file is composed of many different parameters; the values assigned to those parameters can be seen or modified using the following commands:

→ `GET DATABASE MANAGER CONFIGURATION`
→ `UPDATE DATABASE MANAGER CONFIGURATION`
→ `RESET DATABASE MANAGER CONFIGURATION`

GET DATABASE MANAGER CONFIGURATION

GET
[DATABASE MANAGER | DB MANAGER | DBM]
[CONFIGURATION | CONFIG | CFG]
<SHOW DETAIL>

GET DBM CFG SHOW DETAIL
   Displays detailed information about an instance's
   configuration

UPDATE DATABASE MANAGER CONFIGURATION

UPDATE
[DATABASE MANAGER | DB MANAGER | DBM]
[CONFIGURATION | CONFIG | CFG]
USING [[*KeyWord*] [*Value*] , ...]
<IMMEDIATE | DEFERRED>

UPDATE DBM CFG USING NOTIFYLEVEL 4
   Indicates that DB2 is to collect the maximum amount
   of diagnostic information available and write it to the
   db2diag.log file and the administration notification log
   when warnings or errors occur

RESET DATABASE MANAGER CONFIGURATION

RESET
[DATABASE MANAGER | DB MANAGER | DBM]
[CONFIGURATION | CONFIG | CFG]

RESET DBM CFG
  Resets an instance's configuration; all configuration
  parameters are assigned their original default values

DB2 Administration Server (DAS)

The DAS is a separate server process that operates
independently of, yet concurrently with, all other
instances. The DAS ...

→ Provides remote clients with the information needed
  to establish communications with other instances
→ Allows remote administration of an instance
→ Assists in task (job) management
→ Provides a way to "discover" information about other
  DAS processes, DB2 instances, and DB2 databases

✓ *In DB2 9.7, the Control Center tools and the DAS have
  been deprecated and may be removed at a later date.*

Configuring the DAS

The DAS is configured via the DB2 Administration Server configuration file. This file also consists of several different parameters; the values assigned to those parameters can be seen or modified using the following commands:

→ `GET ADMIN CONFIGURATION`
→ `UPDATE ADMIN CONFIGURATION`
→ `RESET ADMIN CONFIGURATION`

GET ADMIN CONFIGURATION

GET ADMIN
[CONFIGURATION | CONFIG | CFG]

`GET ADMIN CFG`
  Displays information about the DAS's configuration

UPDATE ADMIN CONFIGURATION

UPDATE ADMIN
[CONFIGURATION | CONFIG | CFG]
USING [[*KeyWord*] [*Value*] ,...]

`UPDATE ADMIN CFG USING SCHED_ENABLE OFF`
  Turns the DB2 Task Scheduler OFF

7

RESET ADMIN CONFIGURATION

RESET ADMIN
[CONFIGURATION | CONFIG | CFG]

`RESET ADMIN CFG`
 Resets the DAS configuration; all configuration
 parameters are assigned their original default values

Configuring Databases

The behavior of a DB2 database is controlled, in part,
by a database configuration file. This file also consists
of several different parameters; the values assigned to
those parameters can be seen or modified using the
following commands:

→ `GET DATABASE CONFIGURATION`

→ `UPDATE DATABASE CONFIGURATION`

→ `RESET DATABASE CONFIGURATION`

GET DATABASE CONFIGURATION

GET [DATABASE | DB]
[CONFIGURATION | CONFIG | CFG]
FOR [*DBAlias*]
<SHOW DETAIL>

`GET DB CFG FOR sample SHOW DETAIL`
 Displays configuration information for a database named
 SAMPLE

UPDATE DATABASE CONFIGURATION

UPDATE [DATABASE | DB]
[CONFIGURATION | CONFIG | CFG]
FOR [*DBAlias*]
USING [[*KeyWord*] [*Value*] ,...]
<IMMEDIATE | DEFERRED>

```
UPDATE DB CFG FOR sample
USING LOCKTIMEOUT 1000
```
Sets the amount of time an application will wait to obtain a lock to 1,000 seconds

RESET DATABASE CONFIGURATION

RESET
[DATABASE | DB]
[CONFIGURATION | CONFIG | CFG]
FOR [*DBAlias*]

```
RESET DB CFG FOR sample
```
Resets the configuration for a database named SAMPLE; all configuration parameters are assigned their original default values

The AUTOCONFIGURE Utility

Using information you provide *about a single database*, the AUTOCONFIGURE utility will recommend optimal Database Manager configuration parameter values, database configuration parameter values, and initial buffer pool sizes to use.

Recommendations made can be displayed, or they can be automatically applied to an instance and a database.

The AUTOCONFIGURE Command

AUTOCONFIGURE
USING [[*Keyword*] [*Value*] ,...]
APPLY [DB ONLY | DB AND DBM | NONE]

AUTOCONFIGURE USING MEM_PERCENT 60
APPLY DB ONLY
  Determines the best configuration to use when 60%
  of the available memory will be available for the instance;
  makes changes to the database configuration only

The AUTOCONFIGURE Command (Keywords and Values)

Keyword	Valid values	Explanation
mem_percent	1–100	Percentage of memory to dedicate to the database.
workload_type	simple, complex, mixed	Simple workloads tend to be I/O-intensive and mostly transactions, whereas complex workloads tend to be CPU-intensive and mostly queries.
num_stmts	1–1,000,000	Number of SQL statements per transaction.
tpm	1–200,000	Transactions per minute.
admin_priority	performance, recovery, both	Optimize for better performance (more transactions per minute) or better recovery time?
is_populated	yes, no	Is the database populated with data?
num_local_apps	0–5,000	Number of connected local applications.
num_remote_apps	0–5,000	Number of connected remote applications.
isolation	RR, RS, CS, UR	Maximum isolation level used by applications connecting to this database.
bp_resizeable	yes, no	Are buffer pools resizable?

Self-Tuning Memory Manager (STMM)

When enabled, DB2's self-tuning memory manager (STMM) dynamically distributes available memory resources (as the workload changes) among the following:

→ Buffer pools
→ Package cache
→ Locking memory
→ Sort memory
→ Database shared memory

Enabling STMM

To enable STMM, set the *self_tuning_mem* database configuration parameter to ON and:

→ Set two or more relevant database configuration parameters (*pckcachesz*, *locklist*, or *maxlocks*, and *sheapthres_shr*) to AUTOMATIC.

or

→ Set the *database_memory* database configuration parameter to AUTOMATIC, and set either one other relevant configuration parameter or the size of one buffer pool to AUTOMATIC.

or

→ Set the *sortheap* database configuration parameter to AUTOMATIC.

Obtaining STMM Information

To determine which memory consumers have self-tuning enabled, examine the database's configuration file and the system catalog:

```
GET DB CFG SHOW DETAIL;
SELECT BPNAME FROM SYSIBM.SYSBUFFERPOOLS
    WHERE NPAGES = -2;
```

To obtain information about memory configuration changes made by STMM, examine the memory tuning log files (stmm.*nn*.log) found in the stmmlog directory.

Automatic Maintenance

Beginning with DB2 9, the following maintenance operations can be performed automatically:

→ Database backups
→ Data defragmentation (table and index reorganization)
→ Statistics collection
→ Statistics profiling

To enable automatic maintenance, set the `auto_maint` database configuration parameter to ON. (This is the default.)

Enabling Individual
Automatic Maintenance Features

To enable or disable individual automatic maintenance features, assign the value ON or OFF to the following database configuration parameters:

– `auto_db_backup`	(Default: OFF)
– `auto_tbl_maint`	(Default: ON)
– `auto_runstats`	(Default: ON)
– `auto_stmt_stats`	(Default: OFF)
– `auto_stats_prof`	(Default: OFF)
– `auto_prof_upd`	(Default: OFF)
– `auto_reorg`	(Default: OFF)

Automatic Maintenance Policies

For some operations, a policy (a defined set of rules or guidelines) can be used to specify the automatic maintenance behavior:

→ Database backup operations (*auto_db_backup*)
→ Table and index reorganization (*auto_reorg*)
→ Statistics collection (*auto_runstats*)

The stored procedures **AUTOMAINT_SET_POLICY()** and **AUTOMAINT_SET_POLICYFILE()** can be used to configure the automated maintenance policy for a database.

Utility Throttling

DB2's throttling system allows maintenance utilities to be run concurrently during critical production periods, while keeping their performance impact on production work within acceptable limits. The following can be throttled:

→ Statistics collection
→ Backup operations
→ Rebalancing operations
→ Asynchronous index cleanups

Controlling Utility Throttling

To use utility throttling, perform the following steps:

1. Define an impact policy for all throttled utilities. This is done by assigning a value between 1 and 100 to the `util_impact_lim` Database Manager configuration parameter.

2. Invoke the desired utility with the `UTIL_IMPACT_PRIORITY [Priority]` option specified (where `Priority` is a value between 1 and 100).

Determining Resource Consumption – An Example

If the value 50 is assigned to the `util_impact_lim` Database Manager configuration parameter as follows:

```
UPDATE DBM CFG USING UTIL_IMPACT_LIM 50
```

And if a backup operation is started by executing a command that looks like this:

```
BACKUP DB sample UTIL_IMPACT_PRIORITY 70
```

What percentage of available resources will be consumed by the backup operation?

Answer: *35%*   *(0.7 x 0.5 = 0.35 or 35%)*

Changing the Priority of a Running Utility

To change the impact setting for a utility that is already running, execute the `SET UTIL_IMPACT_PRIORITY` command:

SET UTIL_IMPACT_PRIORITY [*UtilityID*]
TO [*Priority*]

```
SET UTIL_IMPACT_PRIORITY 1 TO 20
```

A value of 100 represents the highest priority; 1 represents the lowest priority. Setting `Priority` to 0 will force a throttled utility to continue running unthrottled; a non-zero value will force an unthrottled utility to continue running in throttled mode.

The LIST UTILITIES Command

To get the ID of a running utility, execute the `LIST UTILITIES` command:

LIST UTILITIES <SHOW DETAIL>

```
LIST UTILITIES
```

```
LIST UTILITIES

ID              = 1
Type            = RUNSTATS
Database Name   = PROD
Description     = krrose.some_table
Start Time      = 03/17/2011 11:54:45.773215
Priority        = 10
```

Using the Task Center to Schedule Maintenance

The Task Center is a GUI tool that lets users organize task flow, schedule frequently occurring tasks, and report the status of tasks that have been completed.

Several individual tasks can be combined to create a *grouping* task, which is then treated as a single task.

✓ *In order to use the Task Center, the TOOLS catalog must be created, either in a new and separate database or in an existing database.*

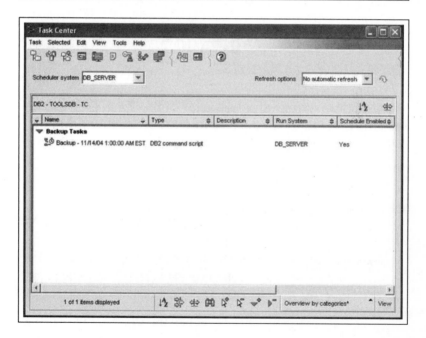

Task Center Operations

Regardless of whether a task completes successfully or fails, when a task has finished, any number of actions can be performed, including:

→ Running another task
→ Scheduling another task
→ Disabling another scheduled task
→ Deleting the task itself

By default, the status of every completed task is recorded in the Journal (which is another GUI tool).

The ADMIN Configuration and the Task Center

To a certain extent, the behavior of the Task Center is controlled through parameters found in the ADMIN configuration file:

→ *toolscat_inst*   TOOLS catalog instance
→ *toolscat_db*   TOOLS catalog database
→ *toolscat_schema* TOOLS catalog schema
→ *sched_enable*   Turns the DB2 Task Scheduler OFF and ON
→ *exec_exp_task*   Specifies whether expired tasks are to be executed (YES or NO) when the DB2 Task Scheduler is turned ON

The Administrative Task Scheduler

Unlike the DB2 Task Scheduler, which is used to automate the execution of *user-defined tasks* (that have been defined via the Task Center), the administrative task scheduler is used to manage and run *administrative tasks* that have been created.

Administrative tasks must be encapsulated in either user-defined or system-defined procedures; you can add, update, and remove tasks from the scheduler's task list by using a set of system-defined procedures: ADMIN_TASK_ADD, ADMIN_TASK_UPDATE, and ADMIN_TASK_REMOVE.

How the Administrative Task Scheduler Works

Scheduled tasks are executed by the DB2 autonomic computing daemon (db2acd), which is started and stopped in conjunction with an instance.

Internally, the daemon maintains a list of active tasks; every five minutes, it connects to each active database and retrieves any new or updated task definitions.

When a task's scheduled execution time arrives, the daemon connects to the appropriate database and calls the procedure associated with the task. (You can obtain information about tasks using two views: ADMIN_TASK_LIST and ADMIN_TASK_STATUS.)

Enabling the Administrative Task Scheduler

The administrative task scheduler is disabled by default. To set up the administrative task scheduler, assign the value YES to the DB2_ATS_ENABLE registry variable and create the SYSTOOLSPACE table space:

```
db2set DB2_ATS_ENABLE=YES;

CREATE TABLESPACE systoolspace
   IN ibmcatgroup
   MANAGED BY AUTOMATIC STORAGE
   EXTENTSIZE 4;
```

What Happens If a Task Takes Longer Than Expected to Run?

The DB2 autonomic computing daemon (db2acd) will not execute a task again if a previous instance of the task is running.

For example, if a task is scheduled to run every 5 minutes and, for some reason, the task takes 6.5 minutes to complete, the daemon will not execute another instance of the task at the next 5-minute interval. Instead, the task will run again at the 10-minute mark.

What Happens If a Task Fails?

If the needed database is not active, the daemon will not execute the task, and a message will be written to both the administration notification log and the DB2 diagnostic log.

If, for some other reason, the daemon fails to execute the task, a message will be written to both logs, and the daemon will attempt to execute the task again every 60 seconds.

Problem Determination

When a problem is encountered, there are several ways to obtain helpful information:

→ The ? command
→ The GET ERROR MESSAGE API
→ First Failure Data Capture (FFDC) output
  – DB2 diagnostic log (db2diag.log)
  – Administration notification log ([*InstanceName*].nfy)
  – Dump files
  – Trap files
  – Core files (Linux and UNIX only)

Controlling First Failure Data Capture (FFDC) Output

To a certain extent, FFDC output is controlled through three Database Manager configuration parameters:

→ *diaglevel*

Controls the type of diagnostic errors that will be recorded in the db2diag log file. Range: 0 (nothing) to 4 (everything)

→ *notifylevel*

Controls the type of messages that will be written to the administration notification log. Range: 0 (nothing) to 4 (everything)

→ *diagpath*

Identifies the fully qualified path where DB2 diagnostic information is stored

DB2 Diagnostic/Administration Notification Log Entry Headers

```
2011-09-19-09.19.51.422000-240 I18037H519         LEVEL: Severe
PID      : 2384               TID  : 2332          PROC : db2syscs.exe
INSTANCE: DB2                 NODE : 000
APPHDL   : 0-50               APPID: *LOCAL.DB2.060919131947
AUTHID   : RSANDERS
FUNCTION: DB2 UDB, data protection services, sqlpgint, probe:1230
RETCODE : ZRC=0x801000A1=-2146434911=SQLP_BACKPEND
          "Backup pending.  Database has been made recoverable.  Backup now required."
          DIA8168C Backup pending for database .
```

The db2diag command can be used to filter and format the contents of the db2diag.log file:

```
db2diag -g level=Severe, pid=2384
```

2

Physical Design

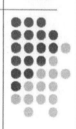

Twenty percent (20%) of the DB2 9.7 for LUW Database Administration Exam is designed to test your ability to create a DB2 9.7 database and to test your knowledge of how data storage is managed.

Simplest Form of the CREATE DATABASE Command

A new database can be created by executing the CREATE DATABASE command. The simplest form of this command is:

CREATE [DATABASE | DB] [*DBName*]

CREATE DATABASE sample
  Creates a new database in the default location, assigns it the name SAMPLE, and configures it to use automatic storage

To override any default behavior, a more complex form of the CREATE DATABASE command must be used.

The CREATE DATABASE Command

```
CREATE [DATABASE | DB] [DBName]
<AUTOMATIC STORAGE [YES | NO]>
<ON [Path] <DBPATH ON [DBPath]>>
<ALIAS [Alias]>
<USING CODESET [CodeSet] TERRITORY [Territory]>
<COLLATE USING [CollateType]>
<PAGESIZE [PageSize]><NUMSEGS [NumSegments]>
<DFT_EXTENT_SZ [DefaultExtentSize]><RESTRICTIVE>
<CATALOG TABLESPACE [TS_Definition]>
<USER TABLESPACE [TS_Definition]>
<TEMPORARY TABLESPACE [TS_Definition]>
<WITH "[Description]">
<AUTOCONFIGURE [AutoConfigOptions]>
```

Default Storage Directory Structure

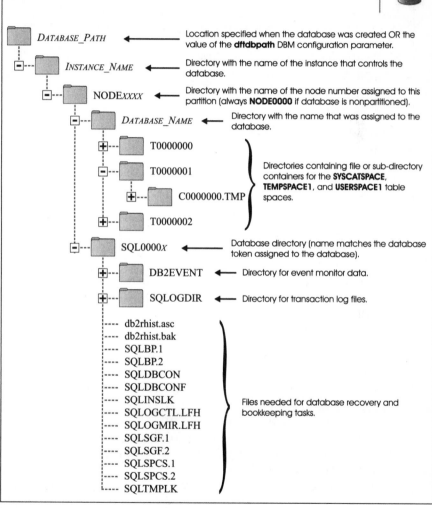

DATABASE_PATH ◄————	Location specified when the database was created OR the value of the **dftdbpath** DBM configuration parameter.
INSTANCE_NAME ◄————	Directory with the name of the instance that controls the database.
NODE*xxxx* ◄————	Directory with the name of the node number assigned to this partition (always **NODE0000** if database is nonpartitioned).
DATABASE_NAME ◄————	Directory with the name that was assigned to the database.
T0000000	
T0000001	Directories containing file or sub-directory containers for the **SYSCATSPACE**, **TEMPSPACE1**, and **USERSPACE1** table spaces.
C0000000.TMP	
T0000002	
SQL0000*x* ◄————	Database directory (name matches the database token assigned to the database).
DB2EVENT ◄—	Directory for event monitor data.
SQLOGDIR ◄—	Directory for transaction log files.

```
---- db2rhist.asc
---- db2rhist.bak
---- SQLBP.1
---- SQLBP.2
---- SQLDBCON
---- SQLDBCONF
---- SQLINSLK
---- SQLOGCTL.LFH
---- SQLOGMIR.LFH
---- SQLSGF.1
---- SQLSGF.2
---- SQLSPCS.1
---- SQLSPCS.2
---- SQLTMPLK
```

Files needed for database recovery and bookkeeping tasks.

Default Authorities Granted to the Database Creator

When a new database is created, the following database authorities are granted to the creator:

→ **DBADM** (Database Administrator)
→ **CONNECT**
→ **CREATETAB**
→ **BINDADD**
→ **CREATE_NOT_FENCED**
→ **IMPLICIT_SCHEMA**
→ **LOAD**

Default Privileges Granted to PUBLIC

If the **RESTRICTIVE** option is not specified, the following authorities/privileges are granted to PUBLIC:

→ **CONNECT**, **CREATETAB**, **BINDADD**, and **IMPLICIT_SCHEMA** on the database
→ **CREATEIN** on schemas **SQLJ** and **NULLID**
→ **USE** on table space USERSPACE1
→ **EXECUTE** on all functions and procedures in schema **SYSIBM**
→ **EXECUTE** with **GRANT** on all functions and procedures in schemas **SQLJ**, **SYSPROC**, and **SYSFUN**
→ **BIND** and **EXECUTE** on all packages in schema **NULLID**
→ **SELECT** on all **SYSIBM** catalog tables, **SYSCAT** catalog views, and **SYSSTAT** catalog views
→ **UPDATE** on all **SYSSTAT** catalog views

Table Spaces

Table spaces are used to control where data for a DB2 database is physically stored and to provide a layer of indirection between database objects and one or more storage containers where the object's data resides. Two types of table spaces can exist:

→ System Managed Space (SMS)
→ Database Managed Space (DMS)

Table Spaces and Automatic Storage

If a database is using automatic storage, another type of table space known as an automatic storage (AS) table space can also exist. Automatic storage tables spaces are just an extension of SMS and DMS table spaces:

→ Regular and large table spaces are created as DMS table spaces.
→ Temporary table spaces are created as SMS table spaces.

Default Table Spaces

When a new database is created, the following table spaces are created by default:

→ One DMS table space named SYSCATSPACE
→ One SMS table space named TEMPSPACE1
→ One DMS table space named USERSPACE1

A buffer pool named IBMDEFAULTBP is also created, and this buffer pool is associated with all of these table spaces.

Table Space Pages and Extents

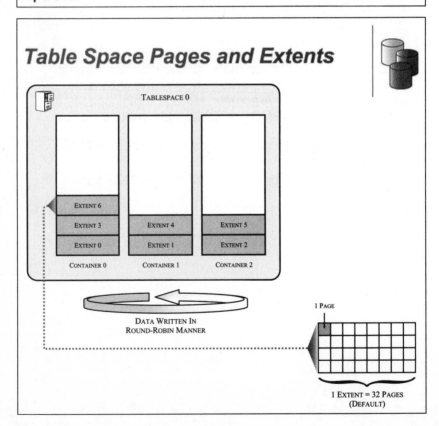

28

How Storage Is Initially Allocated

Each object in a table space allocates storage one page (SMS) or one extent (DMS) at a time. Each object in a DMS table space is also paired with a metadata object called an *extent map*, which describes all of the extents in the table space that belong to the object. Space for extent maps is also allocated one extent at a time.

Therefore, the initial allocation of space for an object in an SMS table space is *1* page; the initial allocation of space for an object in a DMS table space is *2* extents.

How Storage Is Initially Allocated – An Example

```
CREATE TABLESPACE tbsp1 MANAGED BY DATABASE
USING (FILE 'C:\data.dat' 20 M);
CREATE TABLE tab1
  (col1 INT NOT NULL PRIMARY KEY,
   col2 DATE)
  IN tbsp1;
```

2	Extents/object (DMS table space)
X 2	Objects (1 table object and 1 index object)
4	Extents allocated initially

Schemas

A schema is a unique identifier that is used to group a set of database objects:

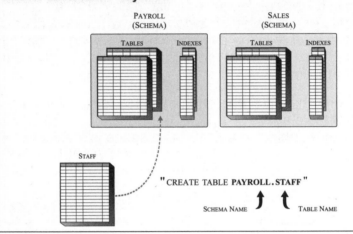

PAYROLL (SCHEMA)   SALES (SCHEMA)

TABLES   INDEXES   TABLES   INDEXES

STAFF

" CREATE TABLE **PAYROLL.STAFF** "

SCHEMA NAME   TABLE NAME

Schemas (Continued)

All data objects (tables, views, indexes, and so on) are created within a schema. If no schema name is provided when an object is created, the name of the user creating the object is used as the schema name — provided the user has IMPLICIT_SCHEMA privileges.

Often, an operation can be performed on all objects in a particular schema by specifying the ON SCHEMA clause with a DB2 command:

REORGCHK UPDATE STATISTICS ON SCHEMA sales

✓ *Some system commands also have a "specific schema" option. For example:*

```
db2look ... -z [Schema ]
db2cat  ... -s [Schema ]
```

Tables

A DB2 database presents data as a collection of tables; a table consists of data that has been logically arranged in columns and rows:

DEPARTMENT TABLE

DEPTID	DEPTNAME	COSTCENTER
A000	ADMINISTRATION	10250
B001	PLANNING	10820
C001	ACCOUNTING	20450
D001	HUMAN RESOURCES	30200
E001	R & D	50120
E002	MANUFACTURING	50220
E003	OPERATIONS	50230
F001	MARKETING	42100
F002	SALES	42200
F003	CUSTOMER SUPPORT	42300
G010	LEGAL	60680

RECORD (ROW)

FIELD (COLUMN)

VALUE

The CREATE TABLE SQL Statement

CREATE TABLE [*TableName*]
([*Column* |
  UniqueConstraint |
  ReferentialConstraint |
  CheckConstraint] , ...)
<LIKE [*Source*] <*CopyOptions* >>
<IN [*TS_Name*]>
<INDEX IN [*TS_Name*]>
<LONG IN [*TS_Name*]>
<PARTITION BY [*PartitionClause*]>
<COMPRESS [YES | NO]>

Defining Columns

[*ColumnName*] [*DataType*]
<NOT NULL>
<GENERATED ALWAYS AS IDENTITY
    <([*IdentityOptions*])>>
<WITH DEFAULT <[*DefaultValue*]] |
    CURRENT DATE |
    CURRENT TIME |
    CURRENT TIMESTAMP>>
<[*UniqueConstraint*] >
<[*CheckConstraint*]>
<[*ReferentialConstraint*]>

A Simple CREATE TABLE Statement

```
CREATE TABLE employee
  (empid INT NOT NULL PRIMARY KEY,
   name   VARCHAR(50),
   sex    CHAR(1) CHECK (sex IN ('M', 'F')),
   dept   INT REFERENCES deptmnt (deptid))
```

Creates a table named EMPLOYEE that has four
columns, a unique constraint, a check constraint, and a
referential constraint that resides in the USERSPACE1
table space

Table Partitioning

Table partitioning is a data organization scheme in which table data is divided across multiple storage objects (data partitions) according to values in one or more columns. Each storage object used can reside in different table spaces, in the same table space, or in a combination of the two.

SALES

| Jan, 2010 | Feb, 2010 | Mar, 2010 | ...... | Nov, 2010 | Dec, 2010 |

Benefits of Table Partitioning

Advantages of using table partitioning include:

→ *Easy roll-in and roll-out of data*
   Data can be rolled in and out by using the ATTACH PARTITION and DETACH PARTITION clauses of the ALTER TABLE statement.
   ✓ *Beginning with DB2 9.7, each partition has its own index, so data partitions can be rolled in and out faster.*

→ *Easier administration of large tables*
   Table-level administration becomes more flexible because administrative tasks (BACKUP, RESTORE, and REORG) can be performed on individual data partitions.

→ *Faster query processing*
   When resolving queries, one or more data partitions may be automatically eliminated based on the predicates used.

Table Partitioning – Automatic Partition Generation

```
<PARTITION BY <RANGE>
  ([ColumnName] <NULLS LAST | NULLS FIRST>,...)
  (STARTING <FROM>
      <(> [Start | MINVALUE | MAXVALUE] <, ...)>
      <INCLUSIVE | EXCLUSIVE>
   ENDING <AT>
      <(> [End | MINVALUE | MAXVALUE] <, ...)>
      <INCLUSIVE | EXCLUSIVE>
   EVERY <(>[Constant] <Duration ><)>
 )>
```

Example of Automatic Partition Generation

```
CREATE TABLE sales
 (sales_date   DATE,
  sales_amt    NUMERIC(5,2))
 IN tbsp0, tbsp1, tbsp2, tbsp3
 PARTITION BY RANGE (sales_date)
    (STARTING '1/1/2010' ENDING '12/31/2010'
     EVERY 3 MONTHS)
```

Creates a table named SALES that is partitioned such that each quarter's data resides in a separate table space

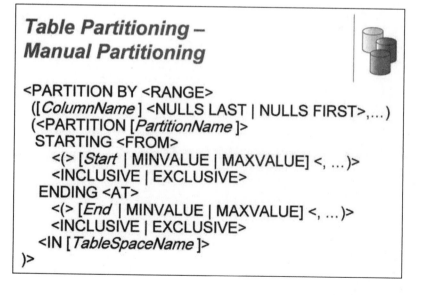

Example of Automatic Partition Generation (Continued)

Q1 Sales	Q2 Sales	Q3 Sales	Q4 Sales

SALES

SALES_DATE between 01/01/2010 and 03/31/2010	SALES_DATE between 04/01/2010 and 06/30/2010	SALES_DATE between 07/01/2010 and 09/30/2010	SALES_DATE between 10/01/2010 and 12/31/2010

TABLE SPACE TBSP0	TABLE SPACE TBSP1	TABLE SPACE TBSP2	TABLE SPACE TBSP3

Table Partitioning – Manual Partitioning

```
<PARTITION BY <RANGE>
  ([ColumnName] <NULLS LAST | NULLS FIRST>,...)
  (<PARTITION [PartitionName]>
    STARTING <FROM>
      <(> [Start | MINVALUE | MAXVALUE] <, ...)>
      <INCLUSIVE | EXCLUSIVE>
    ENDING <AT>
      <(> [End | MINVALUE | MAXVALUE] <, ...)>
      <INCLUSIVE | EXCLUSIVE>
    <IN [TableSpaceName]>
)>
```

Example of Manual Partitioning

```
CREATE TABLE part_table
  (col_1   INT
   col_2   CHAR(3))
  PARTITION BY (col1)
    (STARTING  0 ENDING  9 IN tbsp0,
     STARTING 10 ENDING 19 IN tbsp1,
     STARTING 20 ENDING 29 IN tbsp2,
     STARTING 30 ENDING 39 IN tbsp3)
```

Creates a table named PART_TABLE that is partitioned such that rows with numerical values that fall in the range of 0 to 9 are stored in one table space, rows with numerical values that fall in the range of 10 to 19 are stored in another table space, and so on

Example of Manual Partitioning (Continued)

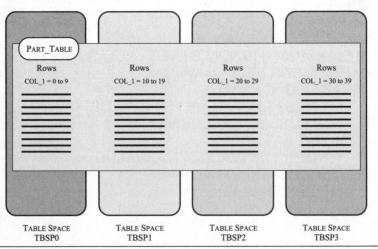

How Storage for a Partitioned Table Is Initially Allocated

```
CREATE TABLESPACE tbsp1 MANAGED BY DATABASE
USING (FILE 'C:\data.dat' 20 M);

CREATE TABLE tab1
  (col1 DATE,
   col2 CHAR(30))
  PARTITION BY RANGE (col1 NULLS FIRST)
   (STARTING '1/1/2009' ENDING '12/31/2009'
    EVERY 3 MONTHS)
  IN tbsp1;
```

```
      2     Extents/object (DMS table space)
  X   4     Objects (1 table object for each partition)
----------
      8     Extents allocated initially
```

Multidimensional Clustering (MDC) Tables

Multidimensional clustering (MDC) provides an elegant method for clustering data in tables along multiple dimensions in a flexible, continuous, and automatic way.

When an MDC table is created, a dimensional key (or keys) along which to cluster the table's data is specified. A dimension block index is then automatically created for each dimension specified and will be used to quickly and efficiently access data along each dimension.

Multidimensional Clustering (MDC) Tables (Continued)

A simple MDC table and its associated indexes:

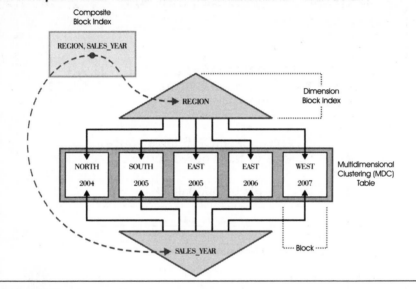

Combining DPF, Clustering, and Partitioning

For ultimate flexibility and maximum performance, you can combine database partitioning, table partitioning, and MDC. Database partitioning will parallelize everything across all database partitions used, while table partitioning and MDC will drastically reduce the I/O required to scan the data and build a result data set.

Tables that take advantage of all of these features can also use local indexes to improve query performance.

Combining DPF, Clustering, and Partitioning (Continued)

Example of all partitioning capabilities being used:

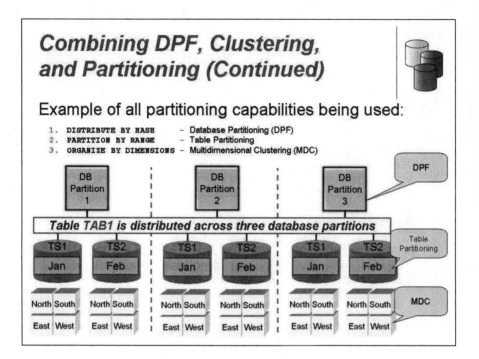

1. `DISTRIBUTE BY HASH` – Database Partitioning (DPF)
2. `PARTITION BY RANGE` – Table Partitioning
3. `ORGANIZE BY DIMENSIONS` – Multidimensional Clustering (MDC)

Table TAB1 is distributed across three database partitions

DB2 pureXML™

The DB2 pureXML™ feature gives a DB2 database the ability to store XML data in its native format while providing it the same levels of security, integrity, and resiliency that are available for relational data.

Anatomy of an XML Document

A well-formed XML document looks similar to this:

```xml
<?xml version="1.0" encoding="UTF-8"?>
<customerinfo xmlns="http://crecord.dat" id="1000">
  <name>John Doe</name>
  <addr country="United States">
    <street>25 East Creek Drive</street>
    <city>Raleigh</city>
    <state-prov>North Carolina</state-prov>
    <zip-pcode>27603</zip-pcode>
  </addr>
  <phone type="work">919-555-1212</phone>
  <email>john.doe@xyz.com</email>
</customerinfo>
```

Anatomy of an XML Document – The XML Declaration

```xml
<?xml version="1.0" encoding="UTF-8"?>
<customerinfo xmlns="http://crecord.dat" id="1000">
  <name>John Doe</name>
  <addr country="United States">
    <street>25 East Creek Drive</street>
    <city>Raleigh</city>
    <state-prov>North Carolina</state-prov>
    <zip-pcode>27603</zip-pcode>
  </addr>
  <phone type="work">919-555-1212</phone>
  <email>john.doe@xyz.com</email>
</customerinfo>
```

Anatomy of an XML Document – Opening and Closing Tags

```
<?xml version="1.0" encoding="UTF-8"?>
<customerinfo xmlns="http://crecord.dat" id="1000">
  <name>John Doe</name>
  <addr country="United States">
    <street>25 East Creek Drive</street>
    <city>Raleigh</city>
    <state-prov>North Carolina</state-prov>
    <zip-pcode>27603</zip-pcode>
  </addr>
  <phone type="work">919-555-1212</phone>
  <email>john.doe@xyz.com</email>
</customerinfo>
```

Anatomy of an XML Document – Attributes

```
<?xml version="1.0" encoding="UTF-8"?>
<customerinfo xmlns="http://crecord.dat" id="1000">
  <name>John Doe</name>
  <addr country="United States">
    <street>25 East Creek Drive</street>
    <city>Raleigh</city>
    <state-prov>North Carolina</state-prov>
    <zip-pcode>27603</zip-pcode>
  </addr>
  <phone type="work">919-555-1212</phone>
  <email>john.doe@xyz.com</email>
</customerinfo>
```

Anatomy of an XML Document – Elements

```
<?xml version="1.0" encoding="UTF-8"?>
<customerinfo xmlns="http://crecord.dat" id="1000">
  <name>John Doe</name>
  <addr country="United States">
    <street>25 East Creek Drive</street>
    <city>Raleigh</city>
    <state-prov>North Carolina</state-prov>
    <zip-pcode>27603</zip-pcode>
  </addr>
  <phone type="work">919-555-1212</phone>
  <email>john.doe@xyz.com</email>
</customerinfo>
```

The XML Data Type

The XML data type is used to define columns in tables that will be used to store XML documents.

To create an XML column in a new table, simply assign the XML data type to a column in a CREATE TABLE or ALTER TABLE SQL statement:

```
CREATE TABLE customer
  (custid    INTEGER NOT NULL,
   custinfo XML)

ALTER TABLE customer
  ADD COLUMN custinfo XML
```

XML Column Restrictions

An XML column has the following restrictions:

→ It cannot be part of any index except an XML index. Therefore, it cannot be part of a primary key or unique constraint.

→ It cannot have a default value specified by the `WITH DEFAULT` clause.

→ It cannot be referenced in a check constraint unless the `IS VALIDATED` predicate is used.

→ It cannot be a foreign key of a referential constraint.

XML Column Restrictions (Continued)

An XML column:

→ Cannot be used as the distribution key

→ Cannot be used as a table-partitioning key

→ Cannot be used in a range-clustered table (RCT)

→ Cannot be used to organize a multidimensional clustering (MDC) table

Common XML Functions

Some of the XML-specific built-in functions that are available with DB2 9.7 are:

→ **XMLPARSE ()**

Parses a character string value and returns a well-formed XML document

→ **XMLSERIALIZE ()**

Converts a well-formed XML document into a character string or large object

→ **XMLTEXT ()**

Returns an XML value with a single XQuery text node

Common XML Functions (Continued)

→ **XMLVALIDATE ()**

Performs an XML schema validation operation

→ **XMLQUERY ()**

Returns an XML value from the evaluation of an XQuery expression

→ **XMLTABLE ()**

Returns a result table from the evaluation of an XQuery expression

Deep Compression

Deep compression (formerly known as *data row compression*) uses a static dictionary-based compression algorithm to compress data by rows. Compression is performed by replacing repeating patterns found in the data with shorter symbol strings; a compression dictionary maps the shorter symbols to the patterns that were replaced.

✓ *With DB2 9.7, both indexes and rows can be compressed.*

How Compression Works

EMPLOYEE TABLE

NAME	DEPT	SALARY	CITY	STATE	ZIPCODE
Fred Smith	500	10000	Raleigh	NC	27603
John Smith	500	20000	Raleigh	NC	27603

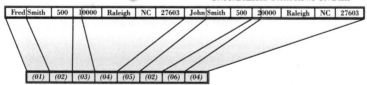

UNCOMPRESSED DATA ROWS ON DISK

| Fred | Smith | 500 | 10000 | Raleigh | NC | 27603 | John | Smith | 500 | 20000 | Raleigh | NC | 27603 |

| (01) | (02) | (03) | (04) | (05) | (02) | (06) | (04) |

COMPRESSED DATA ROWS ON DISK

COMPRESSION DICTIONARY

SYMBOL	PATTERN
01	Fred
02	Smith 500
03	1
04	0000 Raleigh NC 27603
05	John
06	2

Enabling a Table or an Index for Compression

In order to use deep compression, a table or index must be enabled for compression and a compression dictionary must exist. A table or an index can be enabled for compression by executing any of the following commands:

→ `CREATE TABLE ... COMPRESS YES`

→ `ALTER TABLE ... COMPRESS YES`

→ `CREATE INDEX ... <COMPRESS YES>*`

→ `ALTER INDEX [IndexName] COMPRESS YES`

*When you create an index on a table that is already compressed, the new index is compressed immediately.

Creating a Compression Dictionary

Once a table or index has been enabled for compression, a compression dictionary can be created by executing any of the following commands:

→ `REORG TABLE ...`

    `[RESETDICTIONARY | KEEP DICTIONARY] ...`

→ `LOAD ...`

  `REPLACE`

  `[RESETDICTIONARY | KEEP DICTIONARY] ...`

→ `INSPECT ROWCOMPESTIMATE TABLE ...`

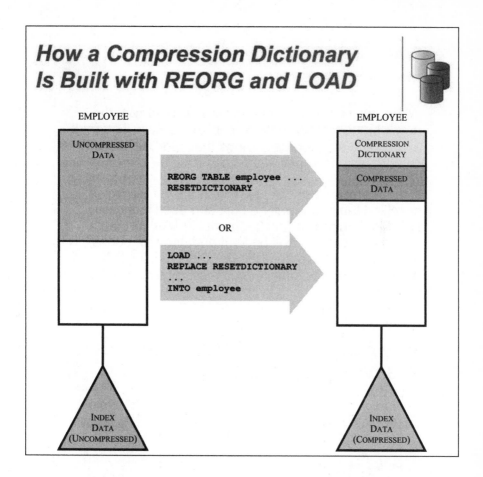

How a Compression Dictionary Is Built with REORG and LOAD

EMPLOYEE

UNCOMPRESSED DATA

REORG TABLE employee ...
RESETDICTIONARY

OR

LOAD ...
REPLACE RESETDICTIONARY
...
INTO employee

EMPLOYEE

COMPRESSION DICTIONARY

COMPRESSED DATA

INDEX DATA (UNCOMPRESSED)

INDEX DATA (COMPRESSED)

The INSPECT Utility and Compression

When the INSPECT command is executed with the ROWCOMPESTIMATE option specified, DB2 will attempt to estimate the storage savings that can be gained by compressing the specified table.

If a compression dictionary does not exist for the specified table, one will be built and used to estimate savings. If the table has been enabled for compression, this dictionary will be kept and used for subsequent compression operations; otherwise, it will be discarded once a compression savings estimate has been determined.

How a Compression Dictionary Is Built with INSPECT

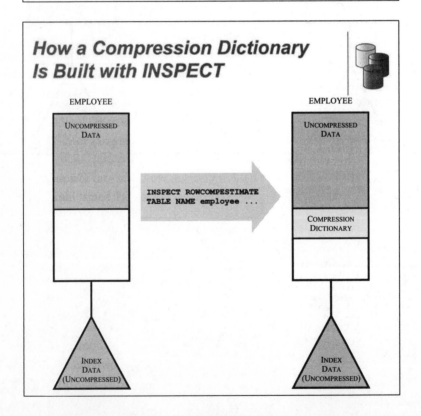

Automatic Dictionary Creation (ADC)

If a table is enabled for compression at the time it is created, a feature introduced in DB2 9.5 called *Automatic Dictionary Creation (ADC)* will cause a compression dictionary to be built automatically as soon as a sufficient amount of data has been stored in the table.

The threshold at which ADC kicks in and begins constructing the compression dictionary is dependent upon the table's row size and how many records have been stored in it; at a minimum, at least 700KB of data must be present in a table before a compression dictionary can be built.

How Automatic Dictionary Creation (ADC) Works

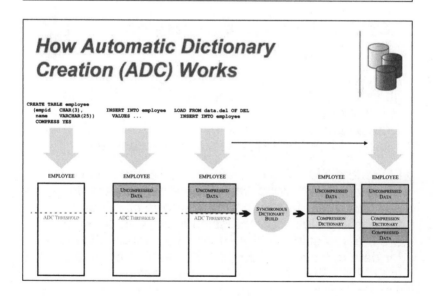

Obtaining Information About the Effects of Compression

Two table functions are available to aid in evaluating the effects of deep compression on a table or an index:

➔ `ADMIN_GET_TAB_COMPRESS_INFO_V97()`

Returns compression information for tables, materialized query tables (MQT), and hierarchy tables

➔ `ADMIN_GET_INDEX_COMPRESS_INFO()`

Returns the potential index compression savings for uncompressed indexes OR reports the index compression statistics from the catalogs

LOBs, XML, and Compression

Large objects (LOBs) and XML documents are generally stored in a location separate from the table row that references them. However, you can choose to store a LOB or XML document (up to 32KB in size) inline in a base table row to simplify access to it.

LOBs and XML documents that are stored inline can be compressed along with other relational data. In addition, XML data in the XML storage object of a table is eligible for compression if the XML columns are created using DB2 9.7 and if you enable the table for data row compression. (XML columns created prior to DB2 9.7 are not eligible for compression.)

3

Business Rules Implementation

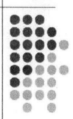

Five percent (5%) of the DB2 9.7 for LUW Database Administration Exam is designed to test your ability to use constraints and views to enforce business rules.

Constraints

Constraints are rules that govern how data values can be added to a table, as well as how those values can be modified. The following types of constraints are available:

→ NOT NULL constraints
→ Default constraints
→ Check constraints
→ Unique constraints
→ Referential integrity constraints
→ Informational constraints

NOT NULL Constraints

A NOT NULL constraint is used to ensure a particular column in a table will never be assigned a null value.

NOT NULL Constraint Example

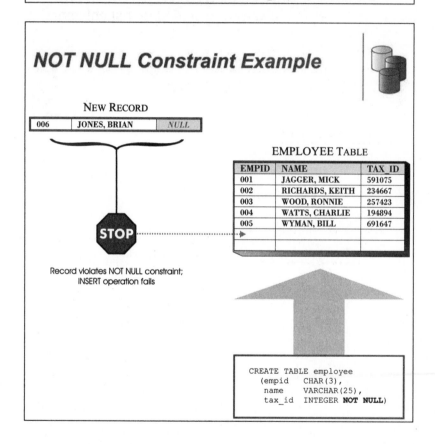

NEW RECORD

| 006 | JONES, BRIAN | NULL |

EMPLOYEE TABLE

EMPID	NAME	TAX_ID
001	JAGGER, MICK	591075
002	RICHARDS, KEITH	234667
003	WOOD, RONNIE	257423
004	WATTS, CHARLIE	194894
005	WYMAN, BILL	691647

STOP

Record violates NOT NULL constraint;
INSERT operation fails

```
CREATE TABLE employee
  (empid   CHAR(3),
   name    VARCHAR(25),
   tax_id  INTEGER NOT NULL)
```

Default Constraints

A default constraint is used to ensure that a default value is always provided for a particular column in a table if no value is explicitly assigned to that column.

Default Constraint Example

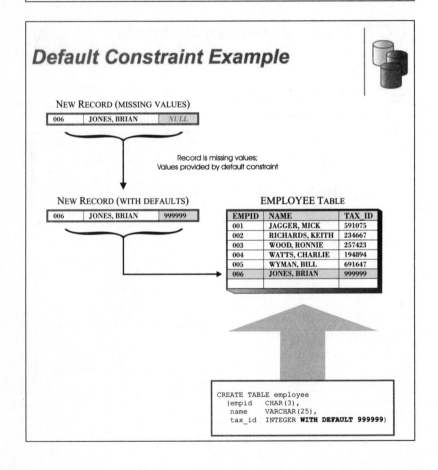

NEW RECORD (MISSING VALUES)

| 006 | JONES, BRIAN | *NULL* |

Record is missing values;
Values provided by default constraint

NEW RECORD (WITH DEFAULTS)

| 006 | JONES, BRIAN | 999999 |

EMPLOYEE TABLE

EMPID	NAME	TAX_ID
001	JAGGER, MICK	591075
002	RICHARDS, KEITH	234667
003	WOOD, RONNIE	257423
004	WATTS, CHARLIE	194894
005	WYMAN, BILL	691647
006	JONES, BRIAN	999999

```
CREATE TABLE employee
  (empid   CHAR(3),
   name    VARCHAR(25),
   tax_id  INTEGER WITH DEFAULT 999999)
```

Check Constraints

A check constraint is used to ensure that the value assigned to a particular column in a table adheres to some business rule.

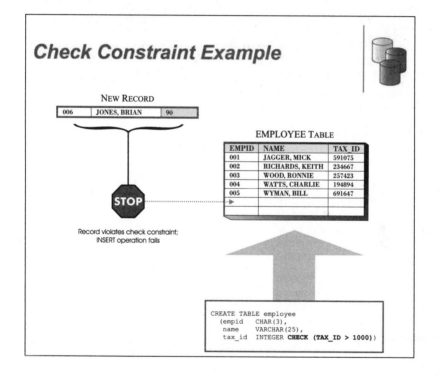

Check Constraint Example

NEW RECORD

| 006 | JONES, BRIAN | 90 |

EMPLOYEE TABLE

EMPID	NAME	TAX_ID
001	JAGGER, MICK	591075
002	RICHARDS, KEITH	234667
003	WOOD, RONNIE	257423
004	WATTS, CHARLIE	194894
005	WYMAN, BILL	691647

STOP

Record violates check constraint;
INSERT operation fails

```
CREATE TABLE employee
  (empid   CHAR(3),
   name    VARCHAR(25),
   tax_id  INTEGER CHECK (TAX_ID > 1000))
```

Unique Constraints

A unique constraint is used to ensure that every value that is assigned to a particular column in a table will be different from all other values that currently exist for the column.

✓ *A primary key is a special unique constraint.*

Unique constraints allow one null value to exist — primary keys cannot contain any null values. Also, multiple unique constraints can exist for a single table, but only one primary key is allowed.

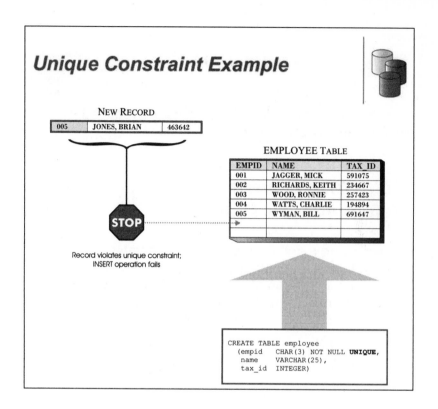

Unique Constraint Example

NEW RECORD

| 005 | JONES, BRIAN | 463642 |

EMPLOYEE TABLE

EMPID	NAME	TAX_ID
001	JAGGER, MICK	591075
002	RICHARDS, KEITH	234667
003	WOOD, RONNIE	257423
004	WATTS, CHARLIE	194894
005	WYMAN, BILL	691647

STOP

Record violates unique constraint;
INSERT operation fails

```
CREATE TABLE employee
   (empid   CHAR(3) NOT NULL UNIQUE,
    name    VARCHAR(25),
    tax_id  INTEGER)
```

Referential Constraints

A referential constraint is used to define required relationships between two base tables.

Rules That Govern Referential Constraints

By enforcing a set of rules that is associated with each referential constraint, DB2 prevents SQL operations that attempt to change data in such a way that referential integrity will be compromised from occurring. This set of rules consists of:

→ An Insert Rule
→ An Update Rule
→ A Delete Rule

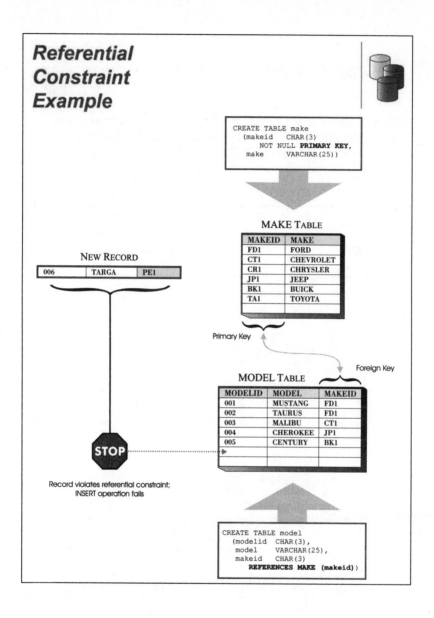

Referential Constraint Example

```
CREATE TABLE make
   (makeid   CHAR(3)
      NOT NULL PRIMARY KEY,
   make      VARCHAR(25))
```

MAKE TABLE

MAKEID	MAKE
FD1	FORD
CT1	CHEVROLET
CR1	CHRYSLER
JP1	JEEP
BK1	BUICK
TA1	TOYOTA

Primary Key

Foreign Key

NEW RECORD

006	TARGA	PE1

MODEL TABLE

MODELID	MODEL	MAKEID
001	MUSTANG	FD1
002	TAURUS	FD1
003	MALIBU	CT1
004	CHEROKEE	JP1
005	CENTURY	BK1

STOP

Record violates referential constraint;
INSERT operation fails

```
CREATE TABLE model
   (modelid   CHAR(3),
   model      VARCHAR(25),
   makeid     CHAR(3)
   REFERENCES MAKE (makeid))
```

The Insert Rule

The Insert Rule guarantees that a value can never be inserted into the foreign key of a child table unless a matching value exists in the corresponding parent key of the associated parent table.

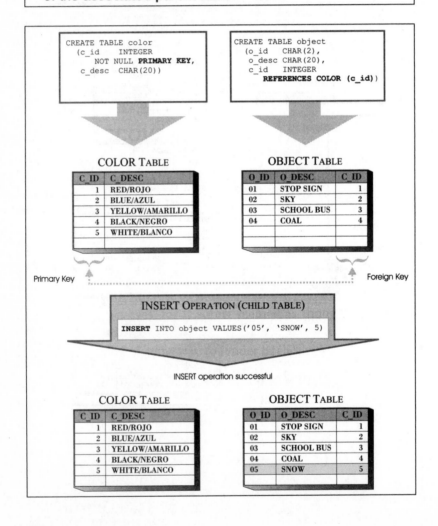

```
CREATE TABLE color
   (c_id    INTEGER
       NOT NULL PRIMARY KEY,
   c_desc  CHAR(20))
```

```
CREATE TABLE object
   (o_id    CHAR(2),
   o_desc  CHAR(20),
   c_id    INTEGER
       REFERENCES COLOR (c_id))
```

COLOR TABLE

C_ID	C_DESC
1	RED/ROJO
2	BLUE/AZUL
3	YELLOW/AMARILLO
4	BLACK/NEGRO
5	WHITE/BLANCO

OBJECT TABLE

O_ID	O_DESC	C_ID
01	STOP SIGN	1
02	SKY	2
03	SCHOOL BUS	3
04	COAL	4

Primary Key

Foreign Key

INSERT OPERATION (CHILD TABLE)

```
INSERT INTO object VALUES('05', 'SNOW', 5)
```

INSERT operation successful

COLOR TABLE

C_ID	C_DESC
1	RED/ROJO
2	BLUE/AZUL
3	YELLOW/AMARILLO
4	BLACK/NEGRO
5	WHITE/BLANCO

OBJECT TABLE

O_ID	O_DESC	C_ID
01	STOP SIGN	1
02	SKY	2
03	SCHOOL BUS	3
04	COAL	4
05	SNOW	5

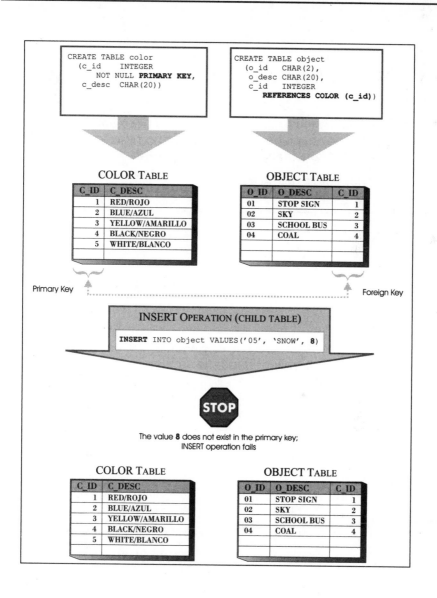

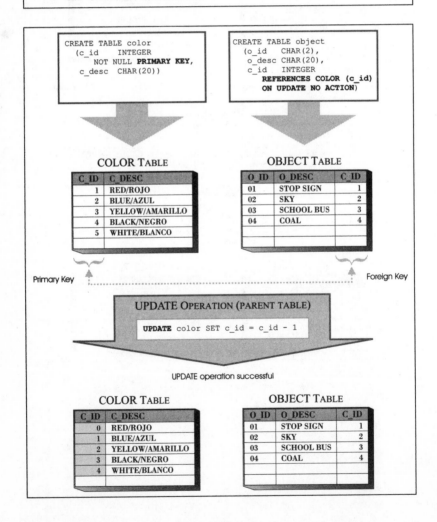

The Update Rule

The Update Rule controls how update operations performed against either table participating in a referential constraint are to be processed.

➜ **ON UPDATE NO ACTION**

➜ **ON UPDATE RESTRICT**

```
CREATE TABLE color
  (c_id    INTEGER
     NOT NULL PRIMARY KEY,
   c_desc CHAR(20))
```

```
CREATE TABLE object
  (o_id    CHAR(2),
   o_desc CHAR(20),
   c_id    INTEGER
     REFERENCES COLOR (c_id)
     ON UPDATE NO ACTION)
```

COLOR TABLE

C_ID	C_DESC
1	RED/ROJO
2	BLUE/AZUL
3	YELLOW/AMARILLO
4	BLACK/NEGRO
5	WHITE/BLANCO

OBJECT TABLE

O_ID	O_DESC	C_ID
01	STOP SIGN	1
02	SKY	2
03	SCHOOL BUS	3
04	COAL	4

Primary Key ⟶ ⟵ Foreign Key

UPDATE OPERATION (PARENT TABLE)

```
UPDATE color SET c_id = c_id - 1
```

UPDATE operation successful

COLOR TABLE

C_ID	C_DESC
0	RED/ROJO
1	BLUE/AZUL
2	YELLOW/AMARILLO
3	BLACK/NEGRO
4	WHITE/BLANCO

OBJECT TABLE

O_ID	O_DESC	C_ID
01	STOP SIGN	1
02	SKY	2
03	SCHOOL BUS	3
04	COAL	4

62

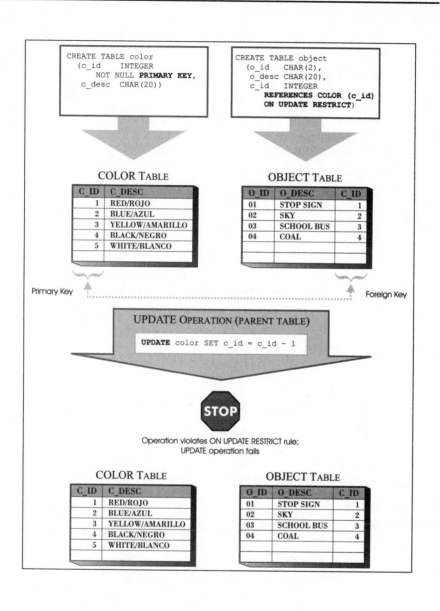

The Delete Rule

The Delete Rule controls how delete operations performed against either table participating in a referential constraint are to be processed.

→ ON DELETE CASCADE
→ ON DELETE SET NULL
→ ON DELETE NO ACTION
→ ON DELETE RESTRICT

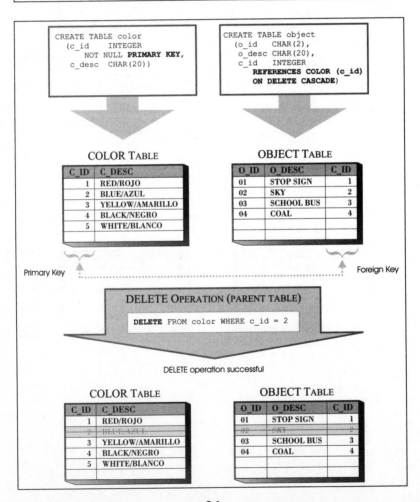

```
CREATE TABLE color
   (c_id    INTEGER
       NOT NULL PRIMARY KEY,
    c_desc  CHAR(20))
```

```
CREATE TABLE object
   (o_id    CHAR(2),
    o_desc CHAR(20),
    c_id    INTEGER
       REFERENCES COLOR (c_id)
       ON DELETE CASCADE)
```

COLOR TABLE

C_ID	C_DESC
1	RED/ROJO
2	BLUE/AZUL
3	YELLOW/AMARILLO
4	BLACK/NEGRO
5	WHITE/BLANCO

OBJECT TABLE

O_ID	O_DESC	C_ID
01	STOP SIGN	1
02	SKY	2
03	SCHOOL BUS	3
04	COAL	4

Primary Key   Foreign Key

DELETE OPERATION (PARENT TABLE)

```
DELETE FROM color WHERE c_id = 2
```

DELETE operation successful

COLOR TABLE

C_ID	C_DESC
1	RED/ROJO
~~2~~	~~BLUE/AZUL~~
3	YELLOW/AMARILLO
4	BLACK/NEGRO
5	WHITE/BLANCO

OBJECT TABLE

O_ID	O_DESC	C_ID
01	STOP SIGN	1
~~02~~	~~SKY~~	~~2~~
03	SCHOOL BUS	3
04	COAL	4

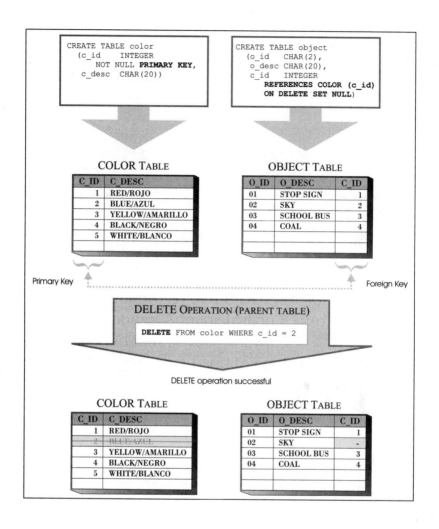

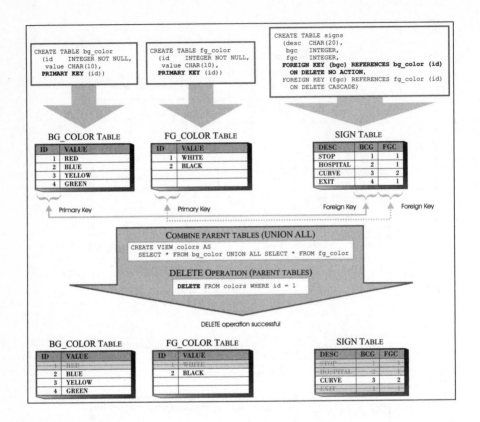

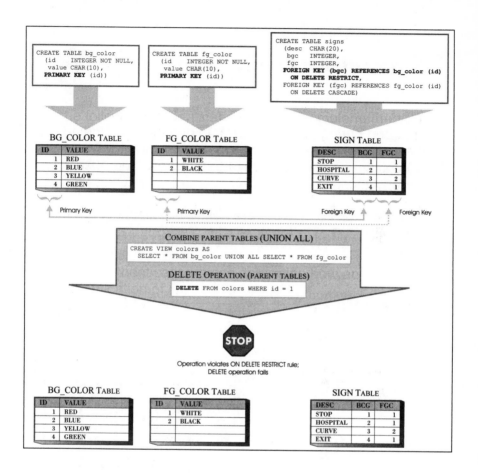

Informational Constraints

Informational constraints are constraints that are *not* enforced during insert and update processing. Instead, they are used to provide information that the DB2 Optimizer can use to improve data access and query performance.

Informational constraints are defined by appending the keywords NOT ENFORCED to the constraint definition.

Informational Constraint Example

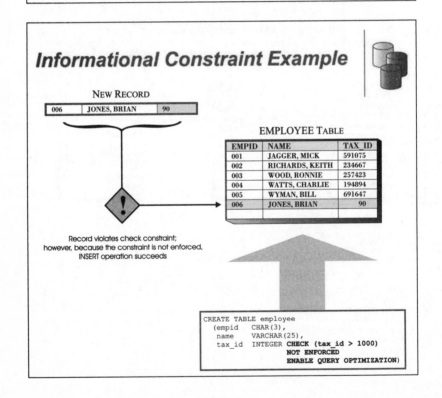

NEW RECORD

| 006 | JONES, BRIAN | 90 |

EMPLOYEE TABLE

EMPID	NAME	TAX_ID
001	JAGGER, MICK	591075
002	RICHARDS, KEITH	234667
003	WOOD, RONNIE	257423
004	WATTS, CHARLIE	194894
005	WYMAN, BILL	691647
006	JONES, BRIAN	90

Record violates check constraint;
however, because the constraint is not enforced,
INSERT operation succeeds

```
CREATE TABLE employee
  (empid   CHAR(3),
   name    VARCHAR(25),
   tax_id  INTEGER CHECK (tax_id > 1000)
           NOT ENFORCED
           ENABLE QUERY OPTIMIZATION)
```

Informational Constraints and Queries

Informational constraints are enforced when queries are executed because the DB2 Optimizer evaluates informational constraints when selecting the best data access plan to use.

✓ *As a result, records that violate an informational constraint may not be seen by some queries.*

Changing the Behavior of Informational Constraints

The behavior of existing check and referential informational constraints can be altered by executing a special form of the `ALTER TABLE` SQL statement:

ALTER TABLE [*TableName*]
ALTER [FOREIGN KEY | CHECK] [*ConstraintName*]
ENABLE QUERY OPTIMIZATION |
DISABLE QUERY OPTIMIZATION |
ENFORCED |
NOT ENFORCED

Temporarily Suspending Constraint Checking

Once a constraint has been defined, data is constantly checked to ensure that the constraint is never violated. However, constraint checking can be turned off and back on using the **SET INTEGRITY** SQL statement.

✓ *Any time constraint checking is disabled for a table, that table is placed in "Check Pending" state and access to it is limited.*

Enforcing Business Rules with Views

Like referential constraints, views can be used to control what values are inserted into a table's columns.

Views can also be used to restrict a user's access to certain columns in a table.

The CREATE VIEW SQL Statement

CREATE VIEW [*ViewName*]
< ([*ColumnName*] ,...) >
AS [*SELECTStatement*]
<WITH <LOCAL | CASCADED> CHECK OPTION>

```
CREATE VIEW view1
   AS SELECT col1, col2
   FROM table1
   WHERE col1 < 5000
   WITH LOCAL CHECK OPTION
```

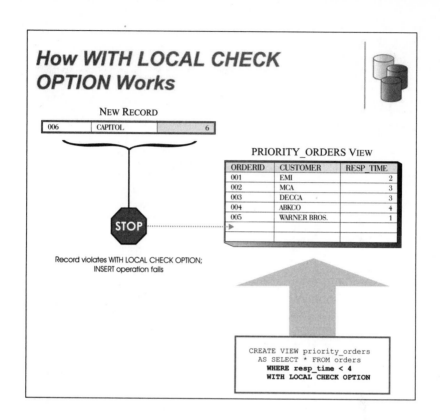

How WITH LOCAL CHECK OPTION Works

NEW RECORD

006	CAPITOL		6

PRIORITY_ORDERS VIEW

ORDERID	CUSTOMER	RESP_TIME
001	EMI	2
002	MCA	3
003	DECCA	3
004	ABKCO	4
005	WARNER BROS.	1

STOP

Record violates WITH LOCAL CHECK OPTION;
INSERT operation fails

```
CREATE VIEW priority_orders
AS SELECT * FROM orders
WHERE resp_time < 4
WITH LOCAL CHECK OPTION
```

71

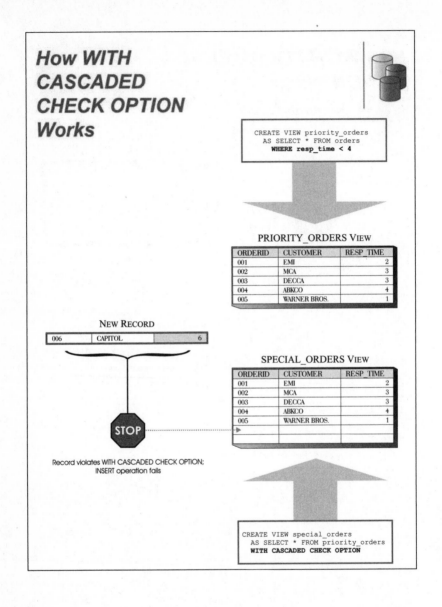

How WITH CASCADED CHECK OPTION Works

```
CREATE VIEW priority_orders
   AS SELECT * FROM orders
   WHERE resp_time < 4
```

PRIORITY_ORDERS VIEW

ORDERID	CUSTOMER	RESP_TIME
001	EMI	2
002	MCA	3
003	DECCA	3
004	ABKCO	4
005	WARNER BROS.	1

NEW RECORD

006	CAPITOL	6

SPECIAL_ORDERS VIEW

ORDERID	CUSTOMER	RESP_TIME
001	EMI	2
002	MCA	3
003	DECCA	3
004	ABKCO	4
005	WARNER BROS.	1

STOP

Record violates WITH CASCADED CHECK OPTION;
INSERT operation fails

```
CREATE VIEW special_orders
   AS SELECT * FROM priority_orders
   WITH CASCADED CHECK OPTION
```

4

Monitoring DB2 Activity

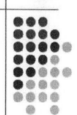

Fifteen percent (15%) of the DB2 9.7 for LUW Database Administration Exam is designed to evaluate your ability to monitor a DB2 server environment using the monitoring tools available with DB2 9.7.

The Database System Monitor

DB2 comes equipped with a built-in monitoring facility known as the Database System Monitor. Although the name implies that this is a single monitoring tool, the Database System Monitor is actually composed of two distinct tools:

→ The Snapshot Monitor
→ Event Monitors

The Snapshot Monitor

The snapshot monitor is designed to collect information about the state of a DB2 instance and the databases it controls *at a specific point in time* (i.e., at the time a snapshot is taken).

To help minimize the overhead involved in collecting snapshot monitor information, a group of switches can be used to control what information is collected when a snapshot is taken.

Snapshot Monitor Switches (And Their Default Settings)

The following snapshot monitor switches are available:

→ **BUFFERPOOL**	OFF
→ **LOCK**	OFF
→ **SORT**	OFF
→ **STATEMENT**	OFF
→ **TABLE**	OFF
→ **TIMESTAMP**	**ON**
→ **UOW**	OFF

Working with Snapshot Monitor Switches

The value assigned to each snapshot monitor switch can be obtained and displayed by executing the GET MONITOR SWITCHES command.

Snapshot monitor switches can be turned on and off at the application level by executing the **UPDATE MONITOR SWITCHES** command.

Snapshot monitor switches can be turned on and off at the instance level by modifying the appropriate snapshot monitor switch Database Manager configuration parameter.

Capturing Snapshot Monitor Data

As soon as a database is activated, the snapshot monitor begins collecting data. But before the data collected can be viewed, a snapshot must be taken.

Snapshots can be taken by executing the GET SNAPSHOT command OR by executing a query that references special administrative views or snapshot monitor table functions. For example:

```
SELECT LOCK_OBJECT_TYPE, LOCK_STATUS
FROM TABLE(SNAP_GET_LOCK('sample', -1))
AS SNAP_INFO
```

Event Monitors

Event monitors are designed to collect information about the state of a database (regarding database activity) *when a specific event or transition occurs*.

Event monitors are database objects; therefore, they are unique to a particular database, and they are created and manipulated using SQL statements.

Event monitors are created by executing the CREATE EVENT MONITOR SQL statement.

Types of Events That Can Be Monitored

With DB2 9.7, event monitors can be created to monitor the following types of events:

→ **DATABASE**　　　　→ **LOCKING***

→ **BUFFERPOOLS**　　　→ **CONNECTIONS**

→ **TABLESPACES**　　　→ **STATEMENTS**

→ **TABLES**　　　　　→ **UNIT OF WORK***

* *Prior to DB2 9.7, it was possible to create* DEADLOCK *(instead of* LOCKING*) and* TRANSACTION *(instead of* UNIT OF WORK*) event monitors.*

Monitoring Deadlocks in DB2 9.7

With earlier releases of DB2, if you wanted to monitor deadlock events, you had to create a DEADLOCKS event monitor and turn it on.

With DB2 9, a **DEADLOCKS** event monitor named DB2DETAILDEADLOCK was created when a new database was created and started when the database was activated.

With DB2 9.7, it is recommended that you use the CREATE EVENT MONITOR FOR LOCKING statement to create an event monitor if you want to monitor deadlock events.

Viewing Event Monitor Data

Data that has been collected by an event monitor can be viewed using one of the following:

→ **The Event Analyzer**

A GUI tool that can be invoked from the Control Center

→ **The Event Monitor Productivity Tool** (db2evmon)

A command-based tool that formats event monitor file and named pipe output and writes it to standard output

→ **The db2evmonfmt tool**

A Java-based, generic XML parser that produces readable flat-text output (text version) or formatted XML output from the data generated by an event monitor

The Event Analyzer

Event Analyzer for CONN_EVENTS

Selected   Help

DB2 - SAMPLE - CONN_EVENTS
Monitored Periods

Connection Time	Start time	Next Connect Time
Aug 19, 2009 10:49:27 PM 725702	Aug 19, 2009 10:53:32 PM 110414	

1 of 1 items displayed   Default View*   View

Navigate to Connections

Close   Help

The Event Monitor Productivity Tool

db2evmon –db [*DatabaseAlias*]
–evm [*EventMonName*]

or

db2evmon –path [*EventMonName*]

```
db2evmon -db sample -evm conn_events
```

The db2evmonfmt Tool

java db2evmonfmt –db [*DatabaseName*]
–ue [*TableName*]
<–u [*UserID*] –p [*Password*]>
[–fxml | –ftext]
<–id [*EventID*]> <–type [*EventType*]>
<–hours [*NumHours*]>
<–w [*WorkloadName*]>
<–a [*AppName*]>
<–s [*SvcSubclass*]>

```
java db2evmonfmt -d sample -ue uow -ftext
```

Monitor Routines and Monitor Elements

A new monitoring infrastructure was introduced with DB2 9.7 that is a superior alternative to the existing database system monitor.

With this new infrastructure, a set of monitor table functions are used to access various monitor elements that are available. These monitor elements provide information about system processing, activities, and data objects, such as tables, table spaces, table space containers, and buffer pools.

DB2 9.7's Monitor Routines

→ MON_GET_ACTIVITY_DETAILS()

Returns detailed monitor metrics about an activity, including general activity information (such as SQL statement text) and a set of metrics for the activity

→ MON_GET_BUFFERPOOL()

Returns monitor metrics for one or more buffer pools

→ MON_GET_CONNECTION()

Returns monitor metrics for one or more connections

→ MON_GET_CONNECTION_DETAILS()

Returns detailed monitor metrics for one or more connections

DB2 9.7's Monitor Routines (Continued)

→ `MON_GET_CONTAINER()`

Returns monitor metrics for one or more table space containers

→ `MON_GET_EXTENT_MOVEMENT_STATUS()`

Returns the status of an extent movement operation

→ `MON_GET_INDEX()`

Returns monitor metrics for one or more indexes

→ `MON_GET_PKG_CACHE_STMT()`

Returns a point-in-time view of both static and dynamic SQL statements in the database package cache

DB2 9.7's Monitor Routines (Continued)

→ `MON_GET_SERVICE_SUBCLASS()`

Returns monitor metrics for one or more service subclasses

→ `MON_GET_SERVICE_SUBCLASS_DETAILS()`

Returns detailed monitor metrics for one or more service subclasses

→ `MON_GET_TABLE()`

Returns monitor metrics for one or more tables

→ `MON_GET_TABLESPACE()`

Returns monitor metrics for one or more table spaces

DB2 9.7's Monitor Routines (Continued)

→ `MON_GET_UNIT_OF_WORK()`

Returns monitor metrics for one or more units of work

→ `MON_GET_UNIT_OF_WORK_DETAILS()`

Returns detailed monitor metrics for one or more units of work

→ `MON_GET_WORKLOAD()` *

Returns monitor metrics for one or more workloads

→ `MON_GET_WORKLOAD_DETAILS()` *

Returns detailed monitor metrics for one or more workloads

* In this case, a workload is a set of transactions.

DB2 Workload Manager

DB2 Workload Manager (WLM) is a comprehensive workload management feature that can help you identify, manage, and control workloads to maximize database server throughput and resource utilization.

WLM is designed to limit the number of disruptive activities that can run concurrently and to stop the execution of activities that exceed predefined boundaries.

✓ *Prior to DB2 9.5, workload management was performed using the DB2 Query Patroller in conjunction with the DB2 Governor.*

DB2 Workload Manager Components

The DB2 Workload Manager architecture consists of the following components:

→ Service classes
→ Workloads
→ Thresholds
→ Work action sets and work class sets

Service Classes

A service class defines an execution environment in which work can be performed; when you define a workload, you indicate the service subclass or superclass where work associated with that workload is to run. Three predefined service superclasses are available:

→ A user service superclass
  (SYSDEFAULTUSERCLASS)
→ A maintenance service superclass
  (SYSDEFAULTMAINTENANCECLASS)
→ A system service superclass
  (SYSDEFAULTSYSTEMCLASS)

Workloads

A workload is a database object that you create to manage different sources of database activities as a group and to prioritize the processing of those activities.

All connections are initially assigned to the default user workload **SYSDEFAULTUSERWORKLOAD**. Connections that are assigned to the default user workload are mapped to the default user service superclass **SYSDEFAULTUSERCLASS**, which provides the default execution environment.

Thresholds

A DB2 WLM threshold is an object that sets a predefined limit over a specific criteria such as consumption of a specific resource or duration of time. There are two types of DB2 WLM thresholds:

→ *Activity thresholds*

> This threshold is triggered when the resource usage of an individual activity violates the activity threshold.

→ *Aggregate thresholds*

> This threshold sets a limit on a measurement across a set of multiple activities and operates as a running total, to which any work tracked by the threshold contributes.

Work Action Sets and Work Class Sets

WLM enables you to treat activities differently based on their activity type or other characteristics. For example, you can treat stored procedures differently from all other read and write operations performed against a database. Such a division is accomplished by using *work action sets*.

Work action sets work hand-in-hand with work class sets. A *work class set* defines the characteristics of the work of interest.

Supported Work Types

A work class has an associated *work type*. The work types recognized by DB2 9.7 are:

Work type	Description
READ	Includes all SELECT and XQuery statements where only data is being fetched (that is, tables are not being updated)
WRITE	Includes all statements that modify data content on the data server (that is, INSERT, UPDATE, DELETE, and MERGE, even if they are embedded in a SELECT statement)
CALL	Includes all invocations of procedures using a CALL statement
DML	Combines work found in the READ and WRITE work types
DDL	Includes statements that create or modify database objects (that is, ALTER, CREATE, COMMENT, DECLARE GLOBAL TEMPORARY TABLE, DROP, GRANT, REFRESH TABLE, RENAME, REVOKE, and SET INTEGRITY)
LOAD	Includes all work initiated by the LOAD utility on the DB2 server
ALL	Includes all types of work

The Explain Facility

The Explain Facility lets you capture and view detailed information about the access plan chosen for a particular SQL statement. This information includes performance data that can be used to identify poorly written queries or a flaw in a database's design.

The Explain Facility uses a special set of tables for data storage. These tables can be created by connecting to a database and running the `EXPLAIN.DDL` script found in the *sqllib/misc* (or *sqllib\misc*) directory.

Types of Explain Data

Two types of Explain data can be collected:

→ **Comprehensive**
  – Contains detailed information about an SQL statement's access plan
  – Information collected is stored across all Explain tables
→ **Snapshot**
  – Contains information about the current internal representation of an SQL statement
  – Information collected is stored in the `SNAPSHOT` column of the `EXPLAIN_STATEMENT` Explain table

Ways to Collect Explain Data

Explain data can be collected by:

→ Executing the EXPLAIN SQL statement
→ Setting the CURRENT EXPLAIN MODE special register
→ Setting the CURRENT EXPLAIN SNAPSHOT special register
→ Using the EXPLAIN precompile/bind option when binding an application
→ Using the EXPLSNAP precompile/bind option when binding an application

Ways to View Explain Data

Once collected, Explain data can be viewed with the following tools:

→ **db2expln**
→ **dynexpln**
→ **db2exfmt**
→ Visual Explain

Visual Explain is a GUI-based tool; the others produce a text-based report that can be displayed on the terminal or written to an ASCII-format file.

Visual Explain

Visual Explain lets users view the details of the access plan that was chosen by the DB2 Optimizer for a given SQL statement. The output provided by Visual Explain consists of a hierarchical graph that represents the various components that are needed to process the access plan chosen for an SQL statement.

✓ *Visual Explain can be used to view only Explain snapshot information; it cannot be used to view comprehensive Explain information.*

Visual Explain (Continued)

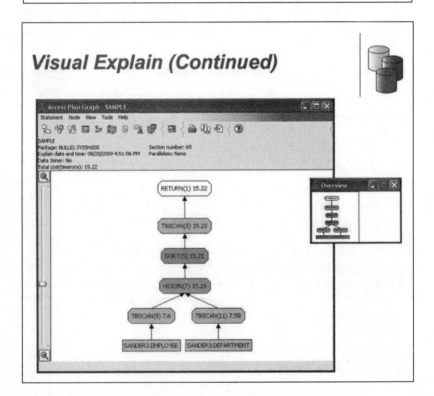

Explainable SQL Statements

The SQL statements for which Explain information can be captured are:

→ `INSERT`
→ `UPDATE`
→ `DELETE`
→ `MERGE`
→ `SELECT`
→ `VALUES`
→ `REFRESH TABLE`
→ `SET INTEGRITY`

Other Useful Monitoring Tools

→ `db2dart`

Examines databases for architectural correctness and reports any errors encountered

→ `db2top`

Provides a unified, single-system view of a single- or multi-partition database by combining snapshot information from each database partition; can be used to collect data about databases, sessions, buffer pools, table spaces, tables, locks, and dynamic SQL

✓ *Only users with* `SYSADM` *authority are allowed to use* `db2dart`; *only users with* `SYSADM`, `SYSCTRL`, `SYSMAINT`, *or* `SYSMON` *authority are allowed to use* `db2top`. *Furthermore,* `db2top` *can be used only on UNIX servers.*

Other Useful Monitoring Tools (Continued)

➙ **db2mtrk**

Provides a complete report of application and database memory usage (the amount of memory allocated to buffer pools and so on)

➙ **db2pd**

Retrieves information from DB2 database system memory sets (such as which databases are active, which indexes are being used to access data, and so on).

✓ *Only users with* SYSADM, SYSCTRL, SYSMAINT, *or* SYSMON *authority are allowed to use* db2mtrk *and* db2pd.

5

Utilities

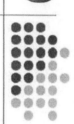

Fifteen percent (15%) of the DB2 9.7 for LUW Database Administration Exam is designed to test your ability to perform common administration tasks using some of the utilities available with DB2.

Data Movement Utilities

The following data movement utilities are available with DB2 9.7:

→ Export
→ Import
→ Load
→ **db2move**

Supported File Formats

DB2's data movement utilities can work with one or more of the following file formats:

→ Delimited ASCII (DEL)
→ Non-delimited or fixed-length ASCII (ASC)
→ Worksheet Format (WSF)
→ PC Integrated Exchange Format (IXF)

Delimited ASCII (DEL)

With this format, data values vary in length, and *delimiters* (unique characters not found in the data values themselves) are used to separate values and rows. Three distinct delimiters are used:

→ Column delimiters (,)
→ Row delimiters (CR/LF)
→ Character value delimiters (")

Delimited ASCII File Example

```
10,"Headquarters",860,"Corporate","New York"
15,"Research",150,"Eastern","Boston"
20,"Legal",40,"Eastern","Washington"
38,"Support Center 1",80,"Eastern","Atlanta"
42,"Manufacturing",100,"Midwest","Chicago"
51,"Training Center",34,"Midwest","Dallas"
66,"Support Center 2",112,"Western","San Jose"
84,"Distribution",290,"Western","Denver"
```

Non-Delimited ASCII (ASC)

With this format, data values have a fixed length, and the position of each value in the file determines which column and row the value belongs to (EXPORT) or is to be assigned to (IMPORT and LOAD).

Non-Delimited ASCII File Example

```
10Headquarters      860CorporateNew York
15Research          150Eastern  Boston
20Legal             40 Eastern  Washington
38Support Center 180 Eastern  Atlanta
42Manufacturing     100Midwest  Chicago
51Training Center 34 Midwest  Dallas
66Support Center 2112Western  San Jose
84Distribution      290Western  Denver
```

Worksheet Format (WSF)

This file format is a special file format that is used exclusively by Lotus 1-2-3 and Lotus Symphony spreadsheet products.

✓ *Support for the WSF file format is deprecated and may be removed in a future release. (New DB2 9.7 tools, such as Optim Data Studio, no longer support the WSF file format.)*

PC Integrated Exchange Format (IXF)

This file format is a special file format that is used almost exclusively to move data between different DB2 databases. With this format, table definitions, table data, and information about all associated indexes is stored in the file. Thus, tables and their corresponding indexes can be created and populated when this file format is used.

Extracting Data from External Files

The file format used determines how data is physically stored in a file; this, in turn, determines the method that must be used to extract data from the file and map it to columns in a table. Three extraction methods are available:

→ The location method (*METHOD L*)
→ The name method (*METHOD N*)
→ The position method (*METHOD P*)

The Location Method (METHOD L)

EMPLOYEE.ASC

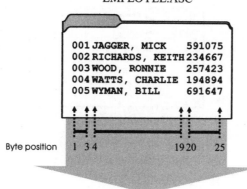

```
001 JAGGER, MICK      591075
002 RICHARDS, KEITH 234667
003 WOOD, RONNIE      257423
004 WATTS, CHARLIE  194894
005 WYMAN, BILL       691647
```

Byte position   1 3 4   19 20   25

EMPLOYEE TABLE

EMPID	NAME	TAX_ID
001	JAGGER, MICK	591075
002	RICHARDS, KEITH	234667
003	WOOD, RONNIE	257423
004	WATTS, CHARLIE	194894
005	WYMAN, BILL	691647

The Name Method (METHOD N)

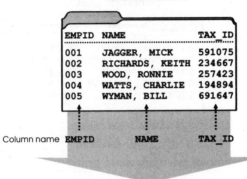

EMPLOYEE.IXF

EMPID	NAME	TAX_ID
001	JAGGER, MICK	591075
002	RICHARDS, KEITH	234667
003	WOOD, RONNIE	257423
004	WATTS, CHARLIE	194894
005	WYMAN, BILL	691647

Column name **EMPID**   **NAME**   **TAX_ID**

EMPLOYEE TABLE

EMPID	NAME	TAX_ID
001	JAGGER, MICK	591075
002	RICHARDS, KEITH	234667
003	WOOD, RONNIE	257423
004	WATTS, CHARLIE	194894
005	WYMAN, BILL	691647

The Position Method (METHOD P)

EMPLOYEE.DEL

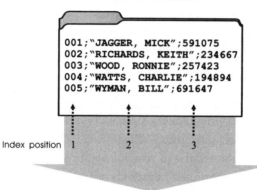

```
001;"JAGGER, MICK";591075
002;"RICHARDS, KEITH";234667
003;"WOOD, RONNIE";257423
004;"WATTS, CHARLIE";194894
005;"WYMAN, BILL";691647
```

Index position   1   2   3

EMPLOYEE TABLE

EMPID	NAME	TAX_ID
001	JAGGER, MICK	591075
002	RICHARDS, KEITH	234667
003	WOOD, RONNIE	257423
004	WATTS, CHARLIE	194894
005	WYMAN, BILL	691647

The Export Utility

The Export utility is used to retrieve data from a DB2 database and copy it to an external file.

The Export utility can be invoked by executing the `EXPORT` command.

The EXPORT Command

EXPORT TO [*FileName*] OF [DEL | WSF | IXF]
<LOBS TO [*LOBPath* , ...]>
<LOBFILE [*LOBFileName* , ...]>
<XML TO [*XMLPath* , ...]>
<XMLFILE [*XMLFileName* , ...]>
<MODIFIED BY [*Modifier* , ...]>
<XMLSAVESCHEMA>
<METHOD N ([*ColumnName* , ...])>
<MESSAGES [*MsgFileName*]>
[*SELECTStatement* | *XQueryStatement*]

Common EXPORT Modifiers

→ **lobsinsepfiles**
→ **xmlinsepfiles**
→ **coldelx**   (coldel;)
→ **chardelx**   (chardel')
→ **decptx**   (decpt,)

✓ *If the* **lobsinsepfiles** *modifier is not used, LOB data is concatenated together in a single file (that is created in the same location as the file containing relational data).*

✓ *Likewise, if the* **xmlinsepfiles** *modifier is not used, XML data is concatenated together in a single file.*

98

Examples of the EXPORT Command

```
EXPORT TO dept.del OF DEL
  MODIFIED BY coldel;
  MESSAGES exp_msgs.txt
  SELECT * FROM department

EXPORT TO C:\data\q12sales.ixf OF IXF
  MESSAGES exp_msgs.txt
  SELECT * FROM q1_sales UNION ALL
    SELECT * FROM q2_sales
```

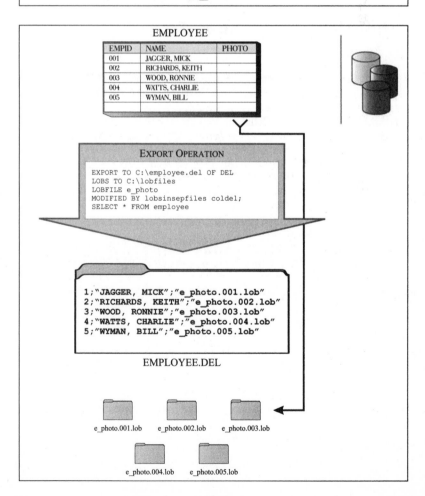

EMPLOYEE

EMPID	NAME	PHOTO
001	JAGGER, MICK	
002	RICHARDS, KEITH	
003	WOOD, RONNIE	
004	WATTS, CHARLIE	
005	WYMAN, BILL	

EXPORT OPERATION

```
EXPORT TO C:\employee.del OF DEL
LOBS TO C:\lobfiles
LOBFILE e_photo
MODIFIED BY lobsinsepfiles coldel;
SELECT * FROM employee
```

```
1;"JAGGER, MICK";"e_photo.001.lob"
2;"RICHARDS, KEITH";"e_photo.002.lob"
3;"WOOD, RONNIE";"e_photo.003.lob"
4;"WATTS, CHARLIE";"e_photo.004.lob"
5;"WYMAN, BILL";"e_photo.005.lob"
```

EMPLOYEE.DEL

e_photo.001.lob   e_photo.002.lob   e_photo.003.lob

e_photo.004.lob   e_photo.005.lob

The Import Utility

The Import utility is used to extract data from an external file and copy it to a DB2 database.

The Import utility can be invoked by executing the `IMPORT` command.

The IMPORT Command

```
IMPORT FROM [FileName] OF [DEL | ASC | WSF | IXF]
<LOBS FROM [LOBPath, ... ]><XML FROM [XMLPath, ... ]>
<MODIFIED BY [Modifier, ... ]><Method>
<XMLPARSE [STRIP | PRESERVE] WHITESPACE>
<XMLVALIDATE USING [XDS [Ignore / Map Options] | SCHEMA
   [SchemaID] | SCHEMALOCATION HINTS]
<ALLOW NO ACCESS | ALLOW WRITE ACCESS>
<COMMITCOUNT [AUTOMATIC | CommitCount]>
<RESTARTCOUNT [RestartCount]>
<MESSAGES [MsgFileName]>
[CREATE | INSERT | INSERT_UPDATE | REPLACE |
   REPLACE_CREATE]
INTO [TableName] <( [ColumnName, ... ] )>
<IN [TSName] <INDEX IN [TSName]><LONG IN [TSName]>>
```

Controlling How the Target Table Is Altered

→ `CREATE`
   Target table is created and populated.
→ `INSERT`
   Data is added to existing target table.
→ `INSERT_UPDATE`
   New data is added to target table; existing data is updated.
→ `REPLACE`
   Existing data is deleted from target table; new data is added (cannot be used if a parent table is the target).
→ `REPLACE_CREATE`
   Target table is created if it does not exist; existing data is deleted before new data is added.

Effects of *ALLOW WRITE ACCESS*

If an import operation is started with the `ALLOW WRITE ACCESS` option specified, users will have full access to the table being populated.

However, the Import utility will attempt to acquire a table-level lock after each commit operation, and this can have a significant negative impact on performance. (During each commit, the Import utility will lose its table-level lock and will try to reacquire it after the commit.)

Effects of
COMMITCOUNT AUTOMATIC

If an import operation is started with the
`COMMITCOUNT AUTOMATIC` option specified, the
Import utility internally determines when a commit
operation needs to be performed. In this case, the
Import utility will commit for either one of two reasons:

→ To avoid running out of active log space
→ To avoid lock escalation (from row level to table level)

Examples
of the IMPORT Command

```
IMPORT FROM dept.ixf OF IXF
  MESSAGES imp_msgs.txt
  CREATE INTO department IN userspace1

IMPORT FROM C:\data\employees.ixf OF IXF
  LOBS FROM C:\lob_data
  MODIFIED BY lobsinfile
  MESSAGES imp_msgs.txt
  INSERT INTO employees
```

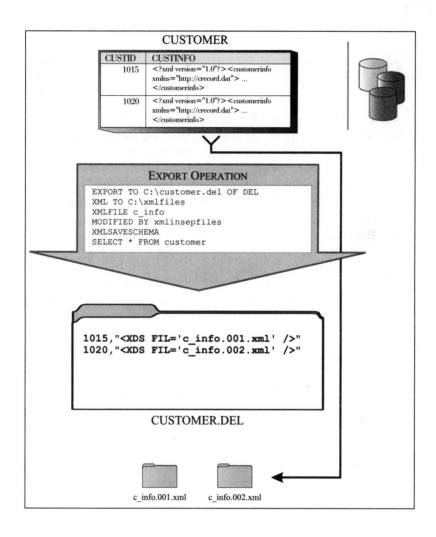

The Load Utility

Like the Import utility, the Load utility can be used to bulk-load data into a database table. However, there are significant differences between the two.

The most important difference is how each utility moves data between an external file and a database; the Import utility copies data using SQL insert/update operations, while the Load utility builds data pages using several rows of data and writes those pages directly to the appropriate table space container(s).

Load Phases

A load operation consists of four distinct phases:

→ The Load phase
→ The Build phase
→ The Delete phase
→ The Index Copy phase

✓ *A "point of consistency" is established between each phase so that if a load operation terminates abnormally, it can be resumed where it left off.*

The LOAD Command

LOAD <CLIENT> FROM [[*FileName*] | [*PipeName*] | [*Device*] | [*CursorName*] , ...] OF [DEL | ASC | IXF]
<LOBS FROM [*LOBPath* , ...]><XML FROM [*XMLPath* , ...]>
<MODIFIED BY [*Modifier* , ...]><*Method* >
<XMLPARSE [STRIP | PRESERVE] WHITESPACE>
<XMLVALIDATE USING [XDS [*Ignore / Map Options*] | SCHEMA [*SchemaID*] | SCHEMALOCATION HINTS]
<SAVECOUNT [*SaveCount*]><ROWCOUNT [*RowCount*]>
<WARNINGCOUNT [*WarnCount*]><MESSAGES [*MsgFileName*]>
[INSERT | REPLACE <KEEPDICTIONARY | RESETDICTIONARY> | RESTART | TERMINATE]
INTO [*TableName*] <([*ColumnName* , ...])>
<FOR EXCEPTION [*ExTableName*]> <STATISTICS [*Options*]>
<NONRECOVERABLE | COPY YES TO [*Location*]>
<WITHOUT PROMPTING> <DATA BUFFER [*Size*]>
<ALLOW NO ACCESS | ALLOW READ ACCESS>
<SET INTEGRITY PENDING CASCADE [IMMEDIATE | DEFERRED]>

Controlling Load Behavior

- **`INSERT`**
  Data is appended to target table (which must already exist).
- **`REPLACE <KEEPDICTIONARY | RESETDICTIONARY>`**
  Existing data is deleted from target table; new data is added. (A new compression dictionary can be built OR an existing compression dictionary can be kept or re-created.)
- **`RESTART`**
  Continues any previous Load operation that failed or was terminated from the last point of consistency.
- **`TERMINATE`**
  Load operation is terminated; new data added is either backed out (**`INSERT`**) or truncated (**`REPLACE`**).

The Purpose of an Exception Table

If a load operation is started and an exception table is not used, any row that is in violation of a unique index or a primary key index will not be loaded, and a warning message will be generated.

If an exception table is used, any row that is in violation of a unique index or a primary key index will be written to the exception table; no warning message will be generated.

Effects of ALLOW READ ACCESS

If a load operation is started with the `ALLOW READ ACCESS` option specified, only data that existed in the table at the time the load operation was started is accessible to other applications; the data being loaded cannot be seen until the load operation is completed.

Examples of the LOAD Command

```
LOAD FROM C:\data\employee.ixf OF IXF
  LOBS FROM C:\lob_data
  MODIFIED BY lobsinfile
  MESSAGES load_msgs.txt
  INSERT INTO employee
  STATISTICS YES
  WITH DISTRIBUTION INDEXES ALL


LOAD FROM /dev/null OF DEL        UNIX
  REPLACE INTO department

LOAD FROM nul OF DEL              Windows
  REPLACE INTO department
```

The db2move Utility

Where the EXPORT, IMPORT, and LOAD commands work with individual tables, the db2move utility can be used to unload and reload an entire database.

When run in EXPORT mode, db2move will scan the system catalog, produce a list of tables, and externalize the data in those tables to IXF-formatted files. When run in IMPORT or LOAD mode, db2move will move data stored in IXF-formatted files into a database, using the list of tables created when run in EXPORT mode.

107

A Word About the db2look Utility

The **db2look** utility will reverse engineer a database and generate DDL statements and DB2 commands that can be used to duplicate a database environment.

The **db2look** utility can also be used to extract the statistics information for a series of database objects and generate **UPDATE** statements that can be used to manually update the statistics in a database.

✓ *The* **db2look** *utility is often used together with the* **db2move** *utility to clone a database.*

Data Maintenance Utilities

Some of the data maintenance utilities available with DB2 9.7 include:

→ **REORGCHK**
→ **REORG**
→ **RUNSTATS**
→ **REBIND**
→ The Design Advisor

The REORGCHK Utility

The REORGCHK utility examines the storage used by a database, generates statistics if appropriate, and analyzes the statistics to determine whether one or more tables need to be reorganized (to remove fragmentation).

The REORG Utility

The REORG utility eliminates gaps in table space containers by retrieving the data stored in a table, ordering it based on one or more of the table's associated indexes, and rewriting the organized data onto unfragmented, physically contiguous pages in storage.

The REORG Command – Tables

REORG TABLE [*TableName*] <INDEX [*IndexName*]>
<ALLOW READ ACCESS | ALLOW NO ACCESS>
<USE [*TmpTSName*] <INDEXSCAN>
<LONGLOBDATA <USE [*LongTSName*]>>
<KEEPDICTIONARY | RESETDICTIONARY>

or

REORG TABLE [*TableName*] <INDEX [*IndexName*]>
<INPLACE> <STOP | PAUSE |
  [ALLOW READ ACCESS | ALLOW NO ACCESS
  <NOTRUNCATETABLE> <START | RESUME>]

The REORG Command – Indexes

REORG INDEXES ALL FOR TABLE [*TableName*]
<ALLOW [READ | WRITE | NO] ACCESS>
<CLEANUP ONLY | CLEANUP ONLY PAGES |
  CLEANUP ONLY ALL | CONVERT>

or

REORG INDEX [*IndexName*]>
<FOR TABLE [*TableName*]>
<ALLOW [READ | WRITE | NO] ACCESS>
<CLEANUP ONLY | CLEANUP ONLY PAGES |
  CLEANUP ONLY ALL | CONVERT>

Examples
of the REORG Command

```
REORG TABLE employee INDEX empno_pk
  USE tbsp1
```

Reorganizes the data in a table named EMPLOYEE,
and cluster its rows based on values in an index
named EMPNO_PK

```
REORG INDEXES ALL FOR TABLE employee
```

Reorganizes the data in all indexes for a table named
EMPLOYEE

The RUNSTATS Utility

The **RUNSTATS** utility collects statistics about tables, indexes, and statistical views; the DB2 Optimizer uses these statistics when selecting an access plan to use for retrieving data in response to a query.

When the RUNSTATS Utility Should Be Used

The **RUNSTATS** utility should be used:

→ When a table has been modified considerably; that is, when 10% to 20% of the data has been affected (e.g., by running the Load utility, with or without the STATISTICS option specified)

→ When a table has been reorganized

→ When a table has been enabled for compression

→ When a new index is created for a table

→ Before binding application programs whose performance is critical

→ When you want to compare current and older statistics

→ When a prefetch quantity is changed

The RUNSTATS Command

RUNSTATS ON TABLE [*TableName*]
<USE PROFILE | UNSET PROFILE | *StatsOptions* >
<ALLOW [READ | WRITE] ACCESS>
<UTIL IMPACT PRIORITY [*Priority*]>

```
RUNSTATS ON TABLE employees
ALLOW READ ACCESS
```

Updates statistics for a table named EMPLOYEES

The REBIND Utility

The **REBIND** utility lets a user re-create a package stored in the database without requiring the original bind file.

The **REBIND** utility also gives users control over when invalid packages are rebound. Invalid packages are automatically (or implicitly) rebound by the DB2 Database Manager when they are executed; it may be desirable to explicitly rebind invalid packages to speed things up and to prevent unexpected SQL error messages (which might be returned in case an implicit rebind fails).

The Design Advisor

Using database statistics and the snapshot monitor or a set of user-supplied SQL statements (known as a *workload*), the Design Advisor recommends indexes and materialized query tables (MQTs) that would improve performance and generates the DDL needed to create those objects.

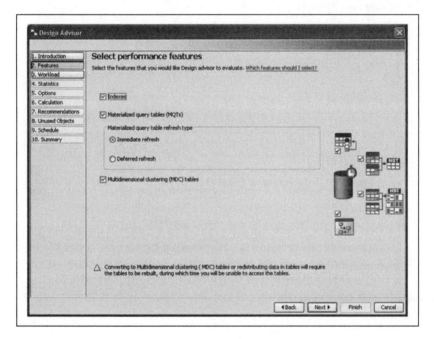

The db2advis Command (Basic Syntax)

```
db2advis -d [DatabaseName]
<-w [WorkloadName]>
<-s "[SQLStatement]">
<-i [InFile]>
<-g>
<-qp [StartTime] <EndTime>
<-a [UserID] <l[Password]>
<-m [AdviseType]>
<-x>
<-u>
<-l [DiskLimit]>
<-t "[MaxAdviseTime]">
<-h>
<-o [OutFile]>
```

Examples of the db2advis Command

```
db2advis -d sample -i db2advis.in
```

Makes recommendations for indexes based on a set of SQL statements and a specification of the frequency at which each statement is to be executed, stored in a file named db2advis.in

```
db2advis -d sample -g
```

Makes recommendations for indexes based on a set of dynamic SQL statements captured by the snapshot monitor

Example of an Input File for the db2advis Command

```
--#SET FREQUENCY 100
SELECT COUNT(*) FROM EMPLOYEE;
SELECT * FROM EMPLOYEE WHERE LASTNAME='HAAS';
--#SET FREQUENCY 1
SELECT AVG(BONUS), AVG(SALARY) FROM EMPLOYEE
    GROUP BY WORKDEPT ORDER BY WORKDEPT;
```

✓ *The* --#SET FREQUENCY *lines indicate the number of times the SQL statements that follow are to be executed.*

Optim Database Administrator

Optim Database Administrator improves productivity and reduces application outages for complex structural changes to streamline change-in-place and database migration scenarios.

Optim Database Administrator includes most of the functions of the Control Center, including table space, table, view, and other object administration and the ability to run utilities such as RUNSTATS, Backup, Export, and Load. Optim Database Administrator also lets you synchronize, copy, or merge schema definitions between DB2 Data Servers.

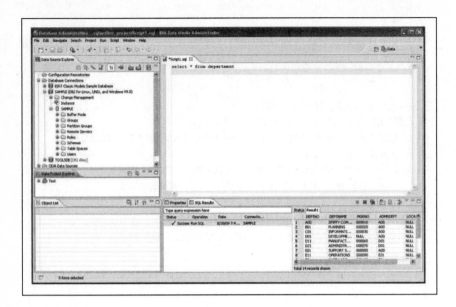

6

High Availability

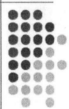

Twenty percent (20%) of the DB2 9.7 for LUW Database Administration Exam is designed to test your ability to back up and restore a database and evaluate your knowledge of High Availability Disaster Recovery (HADR).

Transactions and Transaction Logging

A *transaction* (also known as a *unit of work*) is a sequence of one or more SQL operations grouped together as a single unit, usually within an application process. Two SQL statements are used to terminate a transaction:

→ COMMIT
→ ROLLBACK

Transaction logging is a process that is used to keep track of changes made to a database (by a transaction) *as they are made*.

How Transaction Logging Works

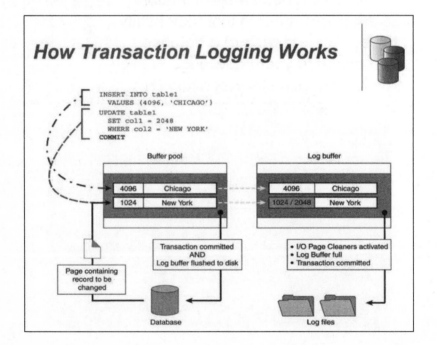

Logging Strategies

Two types of logging strategies are available with DB2:

→ **Circular Logging**
 - Primary log files are reused; secondary log files are used as needed.
 - Roll-forward recovery and user exit program is not supported.
 - A fixed amount of storage space used.

→ **Archival Logging**
 - Log files are used only once.
 - Roll-forward recovery and user exit program are supported.
 - A large amount of storage space is required.

Circular Logging

PRIMARY LOG FILES

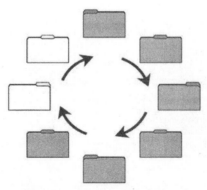

When a primary log file becomes full,
the next file in the sequence is used
(provided it is marked "reusable")

119

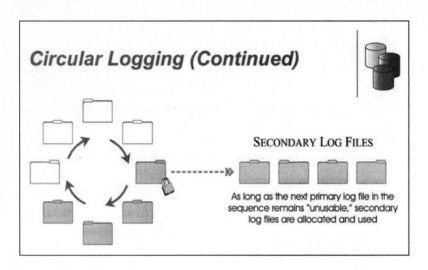

Circular Logging (Continued)

SECONDARY LOG FILES

As long as the next primary log file in the
sequence remains "unusable," secondary
log files are allocated and used

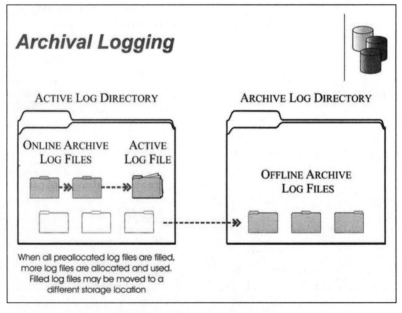

Archival Logging

ACTIVE LOG DIRECTORY

ARCHIVE LOG DIRECTORY

ONLINE ARCHIVE
LOG FILES

ACTIVE
LOG FILE

OFFLINE ARCHIVE
LOG FILES

When all preallocated log files are filled,
more log files are allocated and used.
Filled log files may be moved to a
different storage location

Configuration Parameters That Affect Logging

→ `archretrydelay`

Specifies the amount of time (in seconds) to wait between attempts to archive log files if a previous attempt fails

→ `blk_log_dsk_ful`

Used to prevent disk-full errors from being generated when DB2 cannot create a new log file in the active log path
YES = No error generated

→ `failarchpath`

Specifies an alternate directory to which archive log files are to be written if the preferred log archive method (`logarchmeth1`, `logarchmeth2`) fails

Five attempts are made to archive to the preferred location; logs are archived here if the fifth attempt fails.

Logging Configuration Parameters (Continued)

→ `logarchmeth1, logarchmeth2`

Used to change the logging strategy OR to cause DB2 to store archive log files in a location that is not the active log path

→ `logbufsz`

Sets the amount of memory to use to buffer log records

→ `logfilsiz`

Sets the size, in 4KB pages, of each configured log file

→ `max_log`

Specifies the percentage of primary log space that can be consumed by a single transaction

Logging Configuration Parameters (Continued)

→ `mirrorlogpath`

Specifies a secondary (mirror) log path to which an identical set of log files are to be written

→ `mincommit`

Used to delay the writing of log records to disk until a minimum number of commits has been performed

→ `numarchretry`

Specifies the number of attempts that will be made to archive log files using the specified log archive method before they are archived to the location indicated by `failarchpath`

Logging Configuration Parameters (Continued)

→ `num_log_span`

Sets the number of active log files that an active transaction can span   *0 = Unlimited*

→ `overflowlogpath`

Specifies an alternate location where DB2 is to look for log files needed for a roll-forward recovery operation

→ `logprimary`

Specifies the number of primary log files (of size `logfilsiz`) that are to be created

→ `logsecondary`

Sets the maximum number of secondary log files (of size `logfilsiz`) that are to be created   *−1 = Infinite logging*

Crash Recovery

Crash recovery is performed by using information
stored in the transaction log files to roll back all
incomplete transactions found and complete any
committed transactions that were still in memory (but
had not yet been externalized to the database) when
a failure occurred.

Crash Recovery (Continued)

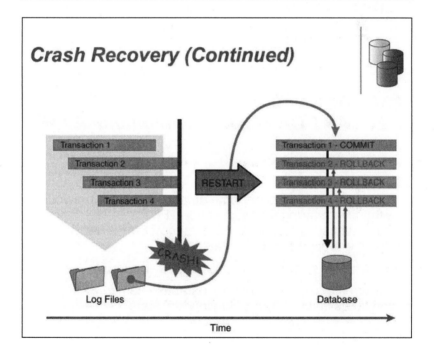

The RESTART DATABASE Command

Crash recovery is performed automatically if the `autorestart` database configuration parameter is set to ON and is performed manually by executing the RESTART DATABASE command:

RESTART [DATABASE | DB] [*DatabaseAlias*]
<USER [*UserName*] <USING [*Password*]>>
<DROP PENDING TABLESPACES
    ([*TS_Name*], ...)>
<WRITE RESUME>

Examples of the RESTART DATABASE Command

RESTART DATABASE sample DROP PENDING
TABLESPACES 'TEMPSPACE1'

Performs crash recovery on a database named SAMPLE without recovering the table space TEMPSPACE1; once the database is restarted, table space TEMPSPACE1 must be dropped and re-created

RESTART DATABASE sample WRITE RESUME

Performs crash recovery on a database named SAMPLE and takes it out of "Write Suspended" state

Version Recovery

Version recovery is performed by replacing the current version of a database with a previous version, using an image that was created with a backup operation; the entire database is rebuilt using a backup image created earlier.

Version recovery is performed by executing the **RESTORE DATABASE** command. Backup images are created by executing the **BACKUP DATABASE** command.

Version Recovery (Continued)

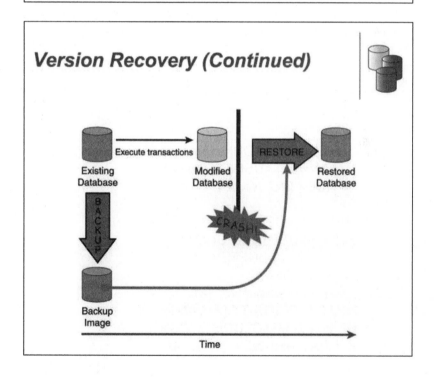

Supported Backup Operations

With DB2, several different types of backup operations can be performed:

→ Offline   (Database shut down during backup)
→ Online   (Database running during backup)

→ Full   (Longest backup time, shortest recovery)
→ Incremental (Medium backup time, medium recovery)
→ Delta   (Shortest backup time, longest recovery)

✓ *A Full backup must be taken before Incremental and Delta backups can be taken.*

The BACKUP DATABASE Command

```
BACKUP [DATABASE | DB] [DatabaseAlias]
<USER [UserName] <USING [Password]>>
<TABLESPACE ( [TS_Name], ... )>
<ONLINE>
<INCREMENTAL <DELTA>>
<TO [Location] | USE SNAPSHOT>
<WITH [NumBuffers] BUFFERS>
<BUFFER [BufferSize]>
<PARALLELISM [ParallelNum]>
<UTIL_IMPACT_PRIORITY [Priority]>
<INCLUDE LOGS | EXCLUDE LOGS>
<WITHOUT PROMPTING>
```

Examples of the BACKUP DATABASE Command

```
BACKUP DATABASE products
  USER db2admin USING ibmdb2
  INCREMENTAL DELTA
  TO /mnt/backups

BACKUP DATABASE finance
  ONLINE TO E:\backups
  UTIL_IMPACT_PRIORITY 15

BACKUP DATABASE sample USE SNAPSHOT
```

Using FlashCopy/Snapshots to Back Up Databases

If a DB2 database is stored on an IBM Storage System (DS8000, N Series, and so on) the BACKUP DATABASE ... USE SNAPSHOT command can be used to back up the database using FlashCopy/Snapshot technology. However, before this technology can be used:

→ DB2 Advanced Copy Services (ACS) must be installed, activated, and configured on the server.
→ DB2 High Availability (HA) features must be available to the server.

The RESTORE DATABASE Command

RESTORE [DATABASE | DB] [*DatabaseAlias*] [CONTINUE |
  ABORT | <USER [*UserName*] <USING [*Password*]>>
  <REBUILD WITH ALL TABLESPACES IN [IMAGE | DATABASE] |
  REBUILD WITH TABLESPACE (*TS_Name*, ...) |
  TABLESPACE <ONLINE> |
  TABLESPACE ([*TS_Name*], ...) <ONLINE> |
  HISTORY FILE <ONLINE> | COMPRESSION LIBRARY | LOGS>
  <INCREMENTAL <AUTO | AUTOMATIC | ABORT>>
  <FROM [*SourceLocation*]] | USE SNAPSHOT>
  <TAKEN AT [*Timestamp*]>
  <TO [*TargetLocation*]> <INTO [*Alias*]> <NEWLOGPATH [*LogPath*]>
  <WITH [*NumBuffers*] BUFFERS><BUFFER [*BufferSize*]>
  <REPLACE EXISTING> <REDIRECT>
  <PARALLELISM [*ParallelNum*]>
  <WITHOUT ROLLING FORWARD> <WITHOUT PROMPTING>]

Examples of the RESTORE DATABASE Command

```
RESTORE DATABASE sample
   USER db2admin USING ibmdb2
   FROM E:\BACKUPS
   REPLACE EXISTING
   WITHOUT PROMPTING

RESTORE DB sample
   USER db2admin USING ibmdb2
   TABLESPACE (tbsp1) ONLINE INCREMENTAL
   FROM E:\BACKUPS

RESTORE DATABASE sample USE SNAPSHOT
```

Creating a New Database from a Backup Image

In addition to facilitating version recovery, the RESTORE DATABASE command can be used to create a new database from a backup image. However, when restoring from one environment to another, some limitations apply:

→ Packages must be rebound before use.

→ SQL procedures must be dropped and re-created.

→ All external libraries must be rebuilt on the new platform.

✓ *These limitations are nonexistent when restoring to a new database in the same environment.*

Roll-Forward Recovery

Roll-forward recovery takes version recovery one step further by replacing the current version of a database with a previous version (stored in a backup image) and replaying information stored in archive log files to return the database to the state it was in at an exact point in time (or at the end of the logs).

Roll-forward recovery is performed by executing the ROLLFORWARD DATABASE command.

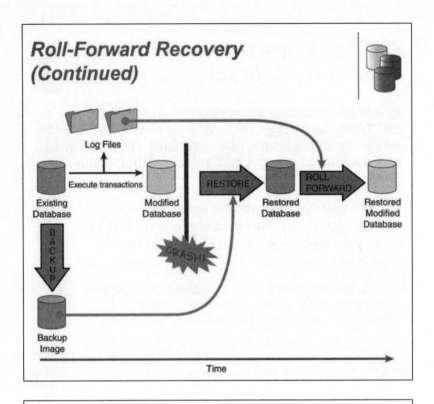

Roll-Forward Recovery (Continued)

Log Files

Execute transactions

Existing Database

Modified Database

RESTORE

Restored Database

ROLL FORWARD

Restored Modified Database

BACKUP

CRASH

Backup Image

Time

Enabling a Database for Roll-Forward Recovery

Although a database can be recovered by performing crash recovery or version recovery, it cannot be restored to a specific point in time unless it has been configured to use archival logging. To switch from circular logging to archival logging, set the `logarchmeth1` database configuration parameter to RECOVERY.

The ROLLFORWARD DATABASE Command

```
ROLLFORWARD [DATABASE | DB] [DatabaseAlias ]
<USER [UserName ] <USING [Password ]>>
<TO [PointInTime ] <USING [UTC | LOCAL] TIME>
   <AND COMPLETE | AND STOP> |
  TO END OF BACKUP <AND COMPLETE | AND STOP> |
  TO END OF LOGS <AND COMPLETE | AND STOP> |
  COMPLETE | STOP | CANCEL |
  QUERY STATUS <USING [UTC | LOCAL] TIME>>
<TABLESPACE <ONLINE> |
   TABLESPACE ( [TS_Name ] , ... ) <ONLINE>>
<OVERFLOW LOG PATH ( [LogDirectory ] , ...)>
<NORETRIEVE>
<RECOVER DROPPED TABLE [TableID ] TO [Location ]>
```

Examples of the ROLLFORWARD DATABASE Command

```
ROLLFORWARD DATABASE payroll
   TO 2011-06-01-00.00.00.0000
   USING LOCAL TIME AND STOP
   OVERFLOW LOG PATH D:\backup_logs

ROLLFORWARD DATABASE sample
   TO END OF LOGS AND STOP
   TABLESPACE (tbsp1)*
```

* If a table space is renamed after a backup image is created, the new name must be used if the table space is referenced in a subsequent ROLLFORWARD DATABASE *command.*

131

The Recover Utility

The Recover utility performs the restore and roll-forward operations needed to recover a database to a specific point in time, based on information found in the recovery history file.

The Recover utility combines the functionality of the RESTORE DATABASE command and the ROLLFORWARD DATABASE command and is invoked by executing the RECOVER DATABASE command.

The RECOVER DATABASE Command

RECOVER [DATABASE | DB] [*DatabaseName*]
<TO [[*PointInTime*] <USING [LOCAL | UTC] TIME] |
    TO END OF LOGS>
<USER [*UserName*] <USING [*Password*]>>
<USING HISTORY FILE ([*HistoryFileName*])>
<OVERFLOW LOG PATH ([*LogPath*])>
<RESTART>

Examples of the RECOVER DATABASE Command

```
RECOVER DATABASE sample
   TO END OF LOGS

RECOVER DB sample
   TO 2011-01-01-00.00.00.0000
   USING LOCAL TIME
   OVERFLOW LOG PATH D:\backup_logs
```

High Availability Disaster Recovery (HADR)

HADR protects against data loss by replicating data changes from a source database, called the *primary*, to a target database, called the *standby*. A database that does not use HADR is referred to as a *standard database*.

The roles of the primary and standby databases can be switched by executing the `TAKEOVER HADR` command — provided the databases are in "peer" state. (The primary and standby databases enter peer state when the standby database receives all of the log files that are on the disk of the primary database server.)

Requirements for Using HADR

Before an HADR environment can be set up:

→ The operating system used on the primary and secondary servers must be the same.
→ The amount of memory available on both servers must be the same.
→ The versions of the DB2 software must be the same.
→ The database path on the primary and secondary servers can be different, but the table spaces and table space containers for both databases must be the same.

Setting Up An HADR Environment

To set up an HADR environment, the following steps must be performed:

→ Back up the database on the primary server.
→ Restore the database on the secondary server.
→ Update the HADR-specific database configuration parameters on each server.
→ Start HADR on the secondary server.
→ Start HADR on the primary server.

Important HADR Configuration Parameters

→ `hadr_local_host`

  Specifies the local host for HADR TCP communications; either a host name or an IP address can be used

→ `hadr_local_svc`

  Specifies the TCP service name or port number for which the local HADR process accepts connections

→ `hadr_remote_host`

  Specifies the TCP/IP host name or IP address of the remote HADR node

→ `hadr_remote_inst`

  Specifies the instance name of the remote server

Important HADR Configuration Parameters (Continued)

→ `hadr_remote_svc`

  Specifies the TCP service name or port number that the remote HADR node will use

→ `hadr_syncmode`

  Specifies how primary log writes are synchronized with the standby database when the systems are in peer state; valid values are `SYNC`, `NEARSYNC`, and `ASYNC`

→ `hadr_timeout`

  Specifies the time (in seconds) that the HADR process waits before considering a communications attempt to have failed

What Gets Replicated

When HADR is set up, the following operations are replicated automatically in the standby database when they are performed at the primary database:

→ Execution of DDL statements
→ Execution of DML statements
→ Buffer pool operations
→ Table space operations and operations on automatic storage databases
→ Table and index reorganizations (online and offline)
→ Import and Load operations
→ Changes to metadata for stored procedures and user-defined functions (UDFs)

Upgrading HADR Servers

To perform a rolling upgrade on a set of HADR servers/databases, complete the following steps:

1. Upgrade the system where the standby database resides.
2. Switch the roles of the primary and standby databases (by executing the TAKEOVER HADR command on the standby server).
3. Upgrade original primary database — which is now the standby database.
4. Switch the roles of the primary and standby database again to return to the original configuration.

7

Security

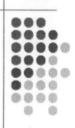

Ten percent (10%) of the DB2 9.7 for LUW Database Administration Exam is designed to test your knowledge of the mechanisms used to control database access and data modification.

Authentication

Access to any DB2 instance or database first requires that the user be *authenticated*. The purpose of authentication is to verify that a user really is who they say they are.

Authentication for DB2 is done using security plug-ins. A security plug-in is a dynamically loadable library that provides authentication security services.

Security Plug-Ins

The DB2 database system provides the following types of security plug-ins:

→ A group retrieval plug-in
→ A client authentication plug-in
→ A server authentication plug-in

The DB2 Database Manager supports two mechanisms for security plug-in authentication:

→ User-ID/password authentication
→ Generic Security Services Application Program Interface (GSS-API) authentication

User ID/Password Authentication

The following authentication types are implemented using user-ID/password authentication plug-ins:

→ `CLIENT`
→ `SERVER`
→ `SERVER_ENCRYPT`
→ `DATA_ENCRYPT`
→ `DATA_ENCRYPT_CMP`

These authentication types determine how and where authentication of a user occurs.

GSS-API Authentication

The following authentication types are implemented using GSS-API authentication plug-ins:

→ `KERBEROS`   (Enabled by default on Windows)
→ `GSSPLUGIN*`
→ `KRB_SERVER_ENCRYPT`
→ `GSS_SERVER_ENCRYPT`

A list of GSS-API plug-ins that a particular server supports is specified in the *`srvcon_gssplugin_list`* Database Manager configuration parameter.

* If `GSSPLUGIN` *is not supported, the authentication type used is equivalent to* `SERVER_ENCRYPT`.

LDAP-Based Authentication

On AIX, you can configure DB2 instances to authenticate users and acquire their groups through the operating system. The AIX operating system will, in turn, perform the authentication through a Lightweight Directory Access Protocol (LDAP) server. To enable transparent LDAP authentication, set the DB2AUTH registry variable to OSAUTHDB.

Authorities and Privileges

Authorities and privileges control what an authenticated user can and cannot do at the system level, database level, and object level. Both can be assigned to individual users, groups of users, or roles.

Authorities and privileges are assigned to users, groups, and roles by individuals who have the authority or privilege to do so.

Instance-Level Authorities

Authorities convey the right to perform high-level tasks against an instance or a database. The following instance-level authorities are available with DB2 9.7:

- System Administrator (SYSADM)
  - System Control (SYSCTRL)
    - System Maintenance (SYSMAINT)
      - System Monitor (SYSMON)

Database-Level Authorities

The following database-level authorities are available with DB2 9.7:

- Security Administrator (SECADM)
  - Access Control (ACCESSCTRL)
  - Data Access (DATAACCESS)
- Database Administrator (DBADM)
  - SQL Administrator (SQLADM)
  - Workload Administrator (WLMADM)
  - Explain Administrator (EXPLAIN)

Object Privileges

Privileges convey the right to perform certain actions against specific database resources. Privileges exist for the following objects:

- Database
- Global variable
- Schema
- Table space
- Table
- View
- Index
- Sequence
- Workload
- Routine
- Package
- Module
- Server
- Nickname
- XSR object
- Role

Roles

A role is a database object that is used to group together one or more authorities/privileges. Once created, a role can be assigned to users, groups, PUBLIC, or other roles.

When roles are used, the assignment of privileges is simplified; instead of granting the same set of authorities/privileges to each individual user in a particular job function, the set of authorities/privileges can be granted to a role representing that job function, and then the role can be granted to each user in that job function.

Granting Authorities and Privileges

There are three different ways that users can obtain authorities and/or privileges:

→ Implicitly   *(When an object is created)*
→ Indirectly   *(When a package is executed)*
→ Explicitly   *(Via the* GRANT *SQL statement)*

The GRANT SQL Statement

The syntax for the GRANT statement looks like this:

GRANT [ALL PRIVILEGES | [*Auth_Privilege* , ...]]
ON [*ObjectType*] [*ObjectName*]
TO [*Recipient*, ...]
<WITH GRANT OPTION>

➔ *Recipient* can be one or more of the following:
- USER [*UserName*]
- GROUP [*GroupName*]
- ROLE [*RoleName*]
- PUBLIC

The GRANT SQL Statement (Continued)

GRANT [**ALL PRIVILEGES** | [*Auth_Privilege, ...*]]
ON [*ObjectType*] [*ObjectName*]
TO [*Recipient, ...*]
< **WITH GRANT OPTION** >

➔ If ALL PRIVILEGES is used, all privileges associated with the specified object *except* CONTROL privilege are granted to the recipient.
➔ If WITH GRANT OPTION is used, the recipient is given the specified privileges, along with the ability to grant those privileges to other users/groups/roles.

The REVOKE SQL Statement

Authorities and/or privileges can be taken from users, groups, and roles by executing the REVOKE statement:

REVOKE [ALL PRIVILEGES | [*Privilege*]]
ON [*ObjectType*] [*ObjectName*]
FROM [*Forfeiter*, ...]

→ *Forfeiter* can be one or more of the following:
- USER [*UserName*]
- GROUP [*GroupName*]
- ROLE [*RoleName*]
- PUBLIC

Example GRANT and REVOKE Statements

```
GRANT USE OF TABLESPACE tbsp1
  TO user1 WITH GRANT OPTION
```
Gives user USER1 the ability to create tables in table space TBSP1 and the ability to grant this privilege to others

```
REVOKE ROLE dev FROM USER user1, USER user2
```
or
```
REVOKE ROLE dev FROM user1, user2
```
Removes users USER1 and USER2 from the DEV role

Label-Based Access Control –
Foundations

According to the *Common Criteria for Information Technology Security Evaluation* international standard (ISO/IEC 15408), there are two ways to control data access:

➔ **Mandatory Access Control (MAC)**
Enforces access control rules based directly on an individual's clearance, authorization for the information being sought, and the confidentiality level of the information being sought.

➔ **Discretionary Access Control (DAC)**
Enforces a consistent set of rules for controlling and limiting access based on identified individuals who "need to know" the information.

DB2's Label-Based Access
Control (LBAC)

DB2's Label-Based Access Control (LBAC) is an implementation of MAC at both the row and the column level. LBAC has the following MAC attributes:

➔ Protected data is assigned a security label.

➔ Only security administrators — not data users — are allowed to make changes to a resource's security label.

➔ Users are given access to any data that is protected by a security label for which they have access, according to the security labels they hold, LBAC rules, and any exemptions they may have.

Setting Up an LBAC Environment

To construct an LBAC-protected system, a user with Security Administrator (**SECADM**) authority must do the following:

1. Create one or more security label components.
2. Create one or more security policies.
3. Create one or more security labels.
4. Grant appropriate security labels to users, groups, and/or roles.

Then, a user with the proper LBAC credentials must associate a security policy with a table to be protected and configure that table for proper protection.

Protecting Rows with LBAC

A table can be configured for row-level LBAC protection by including a column with the **SYSPROC.DB2SECURITYLABEL** data type in the table definition:

```
CREATE TABLE corp.sales (
  sales_rec_id  INTEGER NOT NULL,
  ...
  sec_label SYSPROC.DB2SECURITYLABEL)
SECURITY POLICY sec_policy

ALTER TABLE corp.sales
  ADD COLUMN sec_label DB2SECURITYLABEL
  ADD SECURITY POLICY sec_policy
```

✓ *The table must also be protected by a security policy.*

Protecting Columns with LBAC

A table can be configured for column-level LBAC protection by specifying the `SECURED WITH` option when defining one or more columns:

```
CREATE TABLE hr.employees (
  name VARCHAR(40) SECURED WITH unclassified,
  . . .
 SECURITY POLICY sec_policy

ALTER TABLE hr.employees
 ALTER COLUMN name SECURED WITH unclassified
 ADD SECURITY POLICY sec_policy
```

✓ *Again, the table must also be protected by a security policy.*

Protecting Both Rows and Columns with LBAC

```
CREATE TABLE hr.employees (
  emp_id  INTEGER SECURED WITH classified,
    . . .
  sec_label    DB2SECURITYLABEL)
 SECURITY POLICY sec_policy

ALTER TABLE hr.employees
 ALTER COLUMN emp_id SECURED WITH classified
 ADD COLUMN sec_label DB2SECURITYLABEL
 ADD SECURITY POLICY sec_policy
```

The DB2 Audit Facility

The DB2 audit facility generates, and enables you to maintain, an audit trail for a series of predefined database events. This facility provides the ability to audit at both the instance and the database level.

A user who holds **SYSADM** authority can use the db2audit tool to configure audits at the instance level; a user who holds **SECADM** authority can use audit policies in conjunction with the **AUDIT** SQL statement to configure and control the audit requirements for an individual database.

Audit Facility Stored Procedures

A security administrator (**SECADM**) can use the following audit routines to perform audit tasks:

→ SYSPROC.AUDIT_ARCHIVE()
  Archives audit logs
→ SYSPROC.AUDIT_LIST_LOGS()
  Locates logs of interest
→ SYSPROC.AUDIT_DELIM_EXTRACT()
  Extracts audit data into delimited files for analysis

✓ *The* SECADM *can grant* EXECUTE *privilege on these routines to another user, thereby delegating these tasks.*

8

Connectivity and Networking

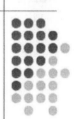

Five percent (5%) of the DB2 9.7 for LUW Database Administration Exam is designed to test your ability to configure database connectivity.

Client/Server Communications

To communicate with a server, clients must use some type of communications protocol that is recognized by the server. Likewise, each server must use some type of communications protocol to detect inbound requests from clients.

The following communications protocols are supported by DB2 9.7's **CATALOG NODE** command:

→ Named pipe
→ TCP/IP (IPv4 and IPv6)

The DB2COMM Registry Variable

Before an instance can actually use a communications protocol, the **DB2COMM** registry variable must be set so that the appropriate communications managers for that protocol will be activated when the instance is started.

The contents of the **DB2COMM** registry variable can be viewed and/or modified with the **db2set** command:

```
db2set -all

db2set -g DB2COMM=TCPIP
```

DB2 Discovery

Once communications between a client and a server have been established, both the server and the database stored on the server must be cataloged on the client before the client can send requests to the remote database for processing.

DB2 Discovery lets you easily catalog a remote server and database without having to know any detailed communications-specific information.

DB2 Discovery Methods Available

→ SEARCH

The *entire* network is searched for valid DB2 servers/ databases and a list of *all* servers, instances, and databases found is returned to the client, along with the communications information needed to catalog and connect to each.

→ KNOWN

The network is searched for a specific server using a specific communications protocol; a list of instances and databases found at that server is returned.

Configuration Parameters That Control DB2 Discovery

→ *discover* → *discover_comm*	Client DBM Configuration
→ *discover* → *discover_comm*	Server DAS Configuration
→ *discover_inst*	Server DBM Configuration
→ *discover_db*	Server DB Configuration

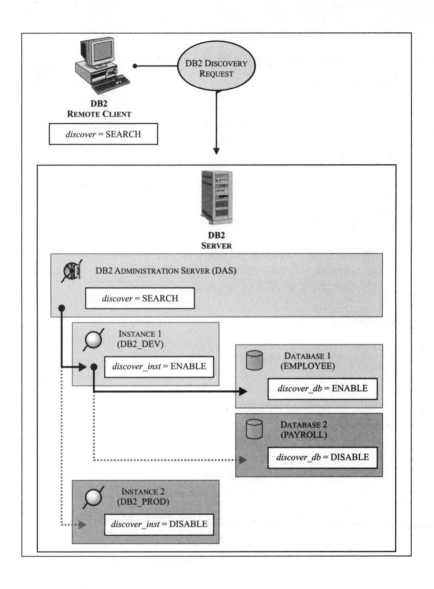

Troubleshooting DB2 Discovery Problems

If you are unable to configure a remote database using DB2 Discovery, see whether you can answer *YES* to all of these questions:

→ Has the `DB2COMM` registry variable been set to the same value on both the client and the server?

→ Does a network connection exist between the client and the server?

→ Have the *discover*, *discover_inst*, and *discover_db* configuration parameters been set appropriately on the client and the server?

Federated Systems

A DB2 *federated system* is a special type of distributed database management system. You can use a federated system to access diverse types of data spread across various data sources (e.g., DB2 for z/OS, Oracle, SQL Server).

Before an instance can communicate with a federated data source, the *federated* Database Manager configuration parameter must to be set to `YES`:

```
UPDATE DBM CFG USING FEDERATED YES
```

Configuring a DB2 Federated System

To configure a federated server to access a DB2 for z/OS data source, you must perform these tasks:

1. Catalog a DB2 node entry.
2. Catalog the remote DB2 database.
3. Register the DB2 wrapper.
4. Register the server definitions for the DB2 data source.
5. Create the user mappings for the DB2 data source.
6. Test the connection to the DB2 data source server.
7. Define nicknames for the DB2 tables and views.

Connectivity and Java Applications

Before SQL statements in any application can be executed, a connection to a database must first be established.

Java applications connect to a DB2 database using the IBM Data Server Driver for JDBC and SQLJ, which is provided with DB2 Connect.

✓ *DB2 Connect is a separate product that requires an additional software license.*

541 Exam Overview

- Exam: 000-541
- Number of questions: 60
- Time allowed: 90 minutes
- Passing score: 61%